6/03

D1401371

RACIAL PROFILING

ABOUT THE AUTHORS

Detective Fredrickson holds a Baccalaureate Degree in Management from Ottawa University, Kansas. He is the co-author of *Applied Police & Fire Photography* (2nd edition), and *Terrorist Attacks* (2nd edition). He has also written several criminal justice articles for various publications. He began his law enforcement career in 1991, and presently serves as a detective with the Drug Enforcement Bureau of the Phoenix Police Department, Phoenix, Arizona. He is a certified instructor with the Arizona Law Enforcement Academy in Street Drugs, Cultural Awareness, and Crime Scene Photography. He speaks to various groups on law enforcement issues.

Mr. Siljander holds a Baccalaureate Degree in Human Services, an Associate Degree in Law Enforcement, an Associate Degree in Fire Science Technology, has completed several specialized courses with private educational institutions, has completed numerous in-service training courses in law enforcement, and he holds the professional designation Associate in Loss Control Management. He has appeared as a speaker for in-service training for law enforcement, and the insurance industry. He is the author and co-author of several technical books: *Applied Surveillance Photography, Applied Police & Fire Photography* (1st & 2nd Edition), *Fundamentals of Physical Surveillance, Terrorist Attacks* (1st & 2nd Edition), *Introduction to Business & Industrial Security and Loss Control, Fundamentals of Civil and Private Investigation, and Private Investigation & Process Serving.* He has also written several law enforcement magazine articles. While in the armed forces, Mr. Siljander served three tours of duty in Vietnam, being honorably discharged in 1972. His diversified occupational history includes a variety of manufacturing and service industries in addition to the insurance industry; industrial security supervision, licensed private investigator doing general and undercover investigations, licensed process server, and local law enforcement as a certified police officer having graduated first in his class in the police academy.

RACIAL PROFILING

Eliminating the Confusion Between Racial and Criminal Profiling and Clarifying What Constitutes Unfair Discrimination and Persecution

By

DARIN D. FREDRICKSON

and

RAYMOND P. SILJANDER

With Forewords by

Loretta Jacobs-Schwartz, Esq.
Civil Rights and Discrimination Attorney

Stephen M. Hennessy, Ed.D.
Training Administrator, Police Department, Phoenix, Arizona

Colonel Dennis A. Garrett
Director, Arizona Department of Public Safety

Charles C Thomas
PUBLISHER • LTD.
SPRINGFIELD • ILLINOIS • U.S.A.

Published and Distributed Throughout the World by

CHARLES C THOMAS • PUBLISHER, LTD.
2600 South First Street
Springfield, Illinois 62794-9265

©2002 by CHARLES C THOMAS • PUBLISHER, LTD.

ISBN 0-398-07255-8 (hard)
ISBN 0-398-07256-6 (paper)

Library of Congress Catalog Card Number: 2001054018

*With THOMAS BOOKS careful attention is given to all details of manufacturing
and design. It is the Publisher's desire to present books that are satisfactory as to their
physical qualities and artistic possibilities and appropriate for their particular use.
THOMAS BOOKS will be true to those laws of quality that assure a good name
and good will.*

*Printed in the United States of America
TH-R-3*

Library of Congress Cataloging-in-Publication Data

Fredrickson, Darin D.
   Racial profiling : eliminating the confusion between racial and criminal profiling and
clarifying what constitutes unfair discrimination and persecution / by Darin D. Fredrickson
and Raymond P. Siljander ; with a foreword by Loretta Jacobs-Schwartz.
      p. cm.
   Includes bibliographical references (p.) and index.
   ISBN 0-398-07255-8 (hard) – ISBN 0-398-07256-6 (pbk.)
   1. Racial profiling in law enforcement--United States. 2. Discrimination in criminal justice administration--United States. 3. Crime and race--United States. I. Siljander, Raymond
P. II. Title.

HV8141 .F7 2002
363.2'3'089–dc21   2001054018

God grant, that not only the love of liberty,
but a thorough knowledge of the Rights of Man,
may pervade all the nations of the Earth,
so that a philosopher may set his foot anywhere
on its surface, and say, "This is my country."

BENJAMIN FRANKLIN

FOREWORD

In this work, the authors tackle one of the most complex and emotionally charged issues presenting law enforcement–and the communities they serve today, that of racial profiling.

Discrimination in today's society takes different forms. Some of it is obvious, but most is invidious, seeping into the interactions of daily life. As the authors point out, however, not all unfair treatment is illegal discrimination. Only that which has either legislatively or judicially declared to be illegal gives the victims of such actions (or inactions) rights protected by law. And, unfortunately, the protection even in those situations can prove insufficient.

Simply put, racial profiling occurs when law enforcement officials rely on race, skin color and/or ethnicity as an indication of criminality, reasonable suspicion, or probable cause, except when part of the description of a particular suspect.[1] Many law enforcement agencies have policies prohibiting racial profiling as unethical and unacceptable conduct. It can also be illegal discrimination, when, as the authors explore, there is no reasonable cause to connect a protected group with the criminal activity the profiling is meant to address.

Racial profiling has become a topic of much discussion, writing, and reporting in the last few years. Certain law enforcement agencies have come under criticism for their actions in implementing and utilizing this tactic. The authors here differentiate between "criminal profiling" and "racial profiling." They define "criminal profiling" as "crime detection wherein police officers are perceptive to various indicators suggesting that someone may be engaged in criminal activity," a practice they defend as legal and necessary in the fight against crime. The authors posit that criminal profiling is often confused with racial profiling, in part because a criminal profile will often include, among other things, race and/or national origin (or some other protected category). While at first blush the two may seem different, in application the line becomes blurred. What a particular individual's "percep-

---

[1] See: Arizona Law Enforcement Racial Profiling Model Policy, Section II "Definitions," May 2001.

tions" are that lead to the suspicion of criminal activity cannot be viewed outside the context of that person's own views of the world. What one police officer thinks is "suspicious" behavior can–and often does–vary from that of another.

The same can be argued with regard to whole communities, as is exemplified by recent headline grabbing stories about racial profiling occurring during "sweeps" of certain geographic areas. Longtime Arizona residents were stopped and asked for documentation (i.e., proof, that they were "legal" residents, not illegal aliens). Many of the stops appeared to have occurred simply because of the person's color, or where they were located at the time. Some law enforcement officers made stereotypic assumptions about the individuals they stopped, again based simply upon skin color or ethnic origin (i.e., that a person of Hispanic appearing heritage speaks only Spanish).

The community was outraged, and divided between those who felt the stops were racially motivated versus those who supported the law enforcement agencies alleged "goals" in taking the actions. Were the actions of the police justified when juxtaposed against the type of crime they were aimed to correct? Do the ends justify the means? What of the frustration of the police officers who daily are on the "front lines" of law enforcement? How do we, as a society, balance those concerns against the community's reaction to such law enforcement activity? These are difficult issues with no clear-cut answers. The effort put forth by the authors in examining these topics, and the suggestions they make to address the problems, is admirable. But it is only a beginning for the reader.

This book will leave you with more questions than answers, more issues than resolutions. It is the goal of the authors that such be the outcome. And, while the authors indicate it is not their intent to exonerate or condemn, but to explore pertinent issues, provide insight, and provoke thought, the reader must continue to be cognizant that each of us–reader, author, civil rights attorney, police officer, minority, community member, etc.–brings to this topic his or her own experiences and belief system.

Having practiced civil rights and discrimination law for over twenty years, I am aware of the difficulty of the task undertaken by this work. I admire Mr. Fredrickson and Mr. Siljander for their efforts–and courage–in treading into this sometimes explosive, but always important issue. The reader will not be disappointed.

LORETTA JACOBS-SCHWARTZ, ESQ.
Scottsdale, Arizona

FOREWORD

The issue of racial profiling is probably one of the most significant and complex issues facing law enforcement today. Most law enforcement and public safety agencies are dealing with the sensitive issue of "driving while Black or Brown" or "DWB."

It has become a controversial topic, one that has and will affect the way law enforcement agencies do business many years into the future. As the authors state, racial profiling is the use of the race of the person viewed as the prime motivator to begin a police action, while criminal profiling is a legitimate method of using race among many other factors in accelerating reasonable suspicion or probable cause. Statistically, more African-Americans will deal in crack cocaine than Whites or Asians. Research also reflects that Whites are more prone to deal in LSD or methamphetamine. The vast majority of serial killers are White.

Herein lies the challenge. What constitutes racial profiling and who makes that determination? How much is the issue of racial profiling going to affect the performance of police agencies throughout the country? In my many years of facilitating discussions with veteran officers about cultural awareness and racial sensitivity, typically the vast majority of attendees to these classes were White, male officers. A typical class would also have only several Black or Hispanic officers in the group. I have always asked this question of the attendees. "Do you think that visible minorities, Black or Brown motorists, are stopped by police for more frivolous reasons that White motorists? In every instance, in both the United States and Canada, the White officers will shake their heads "no" and the minority officers will nod their heads "yes". When I ask the minority officers if they would be willing to describe their experiences, most will comment "It happens all of the time" and go on to explain what happens to them, their wives, husbands, or significant others in interactions with the police. This question and ensuing discussions are very revealing to all of the attendees.

The second question asked is based on the following statement: " I am a White motorist in a Lexus driving in a minority neighborhood known for prostitutes and drug sales. It is two o'clock in the morning. Are you going to stop me?" Half of the attendees no matter what race will say, "Yes, because I know you are up to no good." Half of the attendees will say and rightfully so, they have no right, yet, to stop me, but they will watch me. Are the ones that will stop me profiling me because I am White? What is going on here? Is this a training issue? Are the ranks of the police in the United States full of racists and prejudicial officers? In my thirty-five years of experience in American policing at the federal, state and local levels, I sincerely don't believe this. Does racial profiling exist? It certainly does, but at what level? Is it pervasive in police culture?

These are some of the challenging questions with no simple answers that the authors have begun to address in this book. In this highly emotionally charged topic, the authors begin that long road of trying to address the issues that exist on both sides of the equation. This book reflects a bold step into the realm of the importance of engaging in responsible dialogue without fear of retribution from the "politically correct police." They are true believers that only if people can dialogue with each other and listen to the concerns of each other, then, and only then can we move forward.

The authors bring to this emotion-laden topic the logic of viewing the issues within the social context of the values and practices of the dominant society and the challenges of minority citizens who live in that society. They emphasize that avoiding common errors of logic and reasoning are very important relative to these discussions, particularly in the areas of profiling and discrimination. There is much to be said on both sides of the issue. They explore issues, provide insights, and offer thought provoking and contrasting views on subjects that have often been simplified into ten-second sound bites on the evening news.

In Chapter Six, the authors spend some time in looking at some fascinating areas of the culture of the Gypsies and the sub-cultures of the Hoboes, Tramps, Bums, and Bikers, ones that rarely receive mention in today's society. One can read this area with extreme interest. Another area of great interest is the Criminal Profiling chapter, which is filled with interesting details of effective police practices. The authors speak to the myriad of practices that are an integral part of police work and challenges to those practices that will, no doubt, change the face of policing in this ever-changing multicultural world.

The authors' journey into this emotionally laden and divisive topic of racial and criminal profiling will challenge the reader to think, evaluate, and question as well as grow in knowledge. When we speak, we must speak with knowledge. The authors have done an excellent job in providing knowledge stimulating thought.

STEPHEN M. HENNESSY, ED.D.
Phoenix, Arizona
July 2001

Author's note: Dr. Hennessy is the author of numerous law enforcement/criminal justice magazine articles, and the following books:

Hennessy, Stephen M., Douglas F. Warring, Myrna Cornett-DeVito, James Arnott, and Gerald H. Heuett, (2000), *A CULTURAL AWARENESS TRAINER'S MANUAL FOR LAW ENFORCEMENT OFFICERS*, 5th Ed., Leadership Publishing, Scottsdale, Arizona.

Hennessy, Stephen M., (1999), *THINKING COP FEELING COP: A Study in Police Personalities*, 3rd Ed., Center for Applications of Psychological Type, Inc., Gainesville, Florida.

FOREWORD

Relationships between government and citizens have often been a source of contention and concern. Nowhere are these relationships more prone to incite different reactions than those between citizens and the police. The police: the arm of government empowered to control its citizen's actions, remove their freedom, and in some cases take their very life. On one hand, encouraged to take steps to insure safety and control crime, on the other criticized when issues arise that give concern to police action and tactics.

One such issue that has reached the forefront in recent times is racial profiling, the action of focusing attention on a person not for their alleged criminal actions but because they are of a certain targeted race. There are many views on this issue. Some feel that the issue is perception only. Others feel that it is a rampant procedure tacitly approved by police administrators.

In their book, *Racial Profiling*, Darin Fredrickson and Raymond Siljander review the issue from numerous directions. The information they cite provides a basis to look at the issue of racial profiling as well as criminal profiling. The material presented here will be useful to police administrators as well as students of criminal justice.

COLONEL DENNIS A. GARRETT
Director, Arizona Department of Public Safety
Retired Chief, Phoenix Police Department

PREFACE

This book was written to eliminate confusion regarding what has come to be called racial profiling by clarifying the legitimate law enforcement practice of criminal profiling, and by clarifying what constitutes unfair discrimination, and persecution.

This book was written to benefit sociology students, law enforcement officers, and anyone else in a position to be concerned with, or affected by, the profiling issue. Police administrators, judges, and legislators, must adequately understand the topics and their many ramifications if they are to make decisions that are based on fact rather than stereotype and myth, and free from the influence of adverse social and political pressures. And, attorneys, when prosecuting or defending cases wherein profiling and discrimination is an issue must have good insight into the many interrelated dynamics of the topics to properly prepare and argue their case.

This writing explores difficult social issues that are often poorly understood, but issues that need to be understood if solutions are to be meaningful. And, a poorly conceived solution is especially likely when the issues are both complex and controversial.

In this book the writers acknowledge that while criminal profiling is a necessary and legitimate law enforcement practice, unchecked bias can pollute the practice. And, while they acknowledge that measures to detect those whose enforcement practices reflect bias can have merit, they emphasize that such efforts must be in addition to the hiring of high caliber officers, providing quality training, providing competent leadership, and on a properly staffed and trained Internal Affairs department. But, the authors also emphasize the unfortunate fact that many efforts intended to prevent bias are to varying degrees ineffectual and create collateral problems. Germane to that discussion is illumination of the difficulties of monitoring fair treatment policies, and the unintended problems that often accompany consent decrees.

ACKNOWLEDGMENTS

The authors extend their heartfelt appreciation to the following individuals for generously finding the time to read the manuscript and provide professional, and reader perspective, feedback. Such feedback was essential for an undertaking of this nature. However, it must be emphasized that although they critiqued the manuscript, and offered their views, the contents of this book cannot be considered to represent their personal views and no accountability or blame for anything that is considered to be controversial can be assigned to them. The authors also thank their families for enduring the absence of their loved one while they took time out to provide that valuable and essential contribution. The authors thank:

Dr. Stephen M. Hennessy, Training Administrator,
   Phoenix Police Department.
Shannon L. Lewis, Gang Training Coordinator, Arizona Department
   of Public Safety.
Ariyana Skauge, Arizona Department of Public Safety.
Roger Siljander, Physicist.
Sylvia Wickizer, Private Investigator, Process Server, Realtor.
Tom VanDorn, Detective, Phoenix Police Department.
Reynolds Nejo, police officer, Fort McDowell Tribal Police.
Darius V. Potts, Sergeant, Phoenix Police Department.
Greg Bratt, police officer, Big Lake, Minnesota.

CONTENTS

SECTION I: PROFILING

SECTION II: CULTURAL AWARENESS

RACIAL PROFILING

Section I

PROFILING

Chapter 1

INTRODUCTION

In reality there is no such thing as racial profiling! But, there is such a thing as racial discrimination, and racial persecution. And, racial bias can pollute the legitimate law enforcement practice of criminal profiling.

Prologue

American citizens have constitutional rights, rights guaranteed by the United States Constitution, and state constitutions, with judicial interpretation intended to prevent legislative interference of rights. Many of the restrictions imposed upon law enforcement officers, restrictions that many feel impedes their ability to effectively enforce laws, were imposed with the intention of preventing police abuses or, in other words, to prevent police (and government generally) from infringing upon the constitutionally protected rights of citizens.

It is the effort to ensure against police abuses that police today are concerned with, and governed by, such issues as reasonable suspicion, probable cause, search and seizure laws, having to advise suspects of their rights before questioning, and profiling guidelines. In many instances a good balance has been found between the need to ensure the continued protection of constitutionally protected rights of citizens, and the police having the necessary latitude to perform their job effectively, to protect the citizens without violating their constitutional rights in the process. But, in some instances there seems to be too much or too little control, and periodically a new issue will emerge that calls for resolution by the courts, law makers, and policy makers. How quickly and effectively a new issue is resolved often depends upon its characteristics, and the extent to which it is understood by those who are in policy making positions. That which has come to be called *racial profiling* is one such issue, but the term racial profiling is over used, stigmatized, emotionally charged, clouded with confusion, and frequently applied where there is no relevance.

When the issue of so-called racial profiling emerges, the overriding concern is that of discrimination and persecution, and there is an apparent widespread misunderstanding as to the difference between racial profiling and criminal profiling. And, accepting that racial profiling, as it has come to be understood, is synonymous in many respects with discrimination and persecution, this analysis must of necessity examine the issues of discrimination and persecution. Further, because the very nature of profiling is discriminatory it is also necessary to examine the extent to which discrimination is or is not always wrong.

In this book two forms of so-called "racial profiling" are addressed. One is profiling relative to *Fourth Amendment rights* where police have no legal basis for the enforcement action. The second is profiling relative to *Fourteenth Amendment rights* where police have a legal basis for the enforcement action, but the action is allegedly motivated more by bias than any reasonable suspicion or probable cause that may exist under the circumstances.

The issue called racial profiling has become very problematic for law enforcement. And, unfortunately, for some the term racial profiling also appears to have become a convenient political platform, i.e., if elected I will make racial profiling illegal! How can it be made illegal to do something that does not exist? *In reality there is no such thing as racial profiling! But, there is such a thing as racial discrimination, and racial persecution. And, racial bias can pollute the legitimate law enforcement practice of criminal profiling.* Accepting that it is already illegal to unfairly discriminate against certain classes, and illegal to persecute, intending to enact a law prohibiting "racial profiling" can be argued to be redundant and do little more than create confusion regarding the legitimate law enforcement practice of criminal profiling. The proclaimed intention to make racial profiling illegal tends to suggest either inadequate understanding of the issue and its related dynamics, or an effort to exploit a controversial but badly misunderstood social issue for political reasons. Asserting that one will make racial profiling illegal is reminiscent of the person campaigning for the position of state

Attorney General who emphasized that if elected he would eliminate plea-bargaining. Although as a practical matter that could not be done, and he no doubt knew it, it was intended to appeal to the uninformed for the purpose of capturing votes.

The term racial profiling is invariably used to describe what is felt to be an unfairly discriminatory law enforcement practice that is intrinsically wrong and should never be permitted. But, while it is true that discrimination and persecution is wrong, criminal profiling which may or may not include race among the profiling criteria is not inherently wrong. There is a difference between criminal profiling and that which has come to be called racial profiling although the distinction between the two tends to be misunderstood. And, just because a criminal profile includes race or national origin does not mean it reflects racial bias or will in any way result in discrimination or persecution; it's a question of relevancy. w

Criminal profiling has a legitimate and successful history when applied to such criminals as serial killers, rapists, hijackers, child molesters, and arsonists (Turvey, 1999). Those who are familiar with criminal profiling of serial killers, and child molesters, are aware of the fact that there is a correlation with white males and such crimes. That is a significant observation considering that the racial component of criminal profiling appears to be objectionable only when minorities are identified as being disproportionately involved in certain types of crime such as drug trafficking. In both situations arrest and conviction data provide an empirical basis for inclusion of race or ethnicity in a profile, but do police conduct the same number of traffic stops in America to investigate serial killers and child molesters as they do for drug couriers. The facts would reveal they don't. It may be the sheer number of stops highlighting the distinction and causing a political backlash (Turvey, 1999).

This book is not intended to teach police officers how to do that which is referred to as criminal profiling, although in Chapter 2 considerable space is devoted to clarifying the practice. That is done because unless the practice of criminal profiling is clearly understood, it is impossible to examine it relative to what has come to be called racial profiling. And, such an examination also requires a clear understanding of exactly what constitutes "unfair" discrimination, and persecution, with cultural awareness also being an integral part of the equation. As can be seen, it is a complex issue with many facets.

How the issues of profiling and discrimination are perceived will vary considerably from one class of people to another. How individual police officers view the topics will vary depending on the racial or cultural class to which each officer belongs, and how law enforcement generally views the topics will tend to differ from the manner in which they are viewed by various minorities. Similarly, how a White middle class person views the topics will differ from those groups already mentioned. Members of various subculture groups will also have differing views, as will members of different socioeconomic classes. Naturally, people in positions of power and control will have views that differ from those in subordinate positions.

Generally, people are socialized in a certain environment, in a given circumstance, and that will determine, and limit, how they view the topics and feel about them. However, there are people who have been socialized under circumstances that resulted in their being split between various cultures and/or subcultures and, when that occurs, they are often left with a broader view of the issues. But, while they can view the issues from a broader and varied perspective, they cannot view the issues from all perspectives. And, while the authors have endeavored to discuss the issues in as objective a manner as possible, it must be understood that the issues are highly abstract and subject to numerous points of view and therefore each reader must examine what is presented here and contemplate it relative to their own frame of reference.

Scope, Plan, and Purpose

An understanding of profiling and discrimination requires being able to view the issues within a social context that acknowledges the values and practices of the dominant society, and relative to constitutionally protected rights.

This book was written to eliminate confusion regarding what has come to be called racial profiling by clarifying the legitimate law enforcement practice of criminal profiling, and by clarifying exactly what constitutes unfair discrimination, and persecution. To facilitate that objective, the book features two sections. The first section focuses on profiling issues while the second section features support material. Chapter 2 discusses criminal profiling sufficiently to provide the reader with a clear understanding of that practice. Chapter 3 discusses the difficulties confounding efforts to enact policies and procedures intended to eliminate, or minimize, racial bias when criminal profiling is being done.

The support information in Chapters 4 and 5 is essential to this discussion but features nothing that will be new and exciting for those who have studied psychology and sociology on the college level. However, Chapters 4 and 5 have been included to provide essential key terms and concepts for the benefit of those readers who have not studied psychology and sociology. The information provided in Chapter 6, however, will be interesting and enlightening for most readers and illustrates the extent to which cultures and subcultures are often far more complex and enigmatic than realized, even though the stereotypes applied to them tend to be simplistic and far removed from truth. Chapter 6 has also been included to stimulate cultural awareness and sensitivity, and to stimulate curiosity and a resolve for further study of psychology and sociology, disciplines that are germane to the issue of profiling. It must be remembered that the issue of profiling is, in every respect, a social issue and laws are, in most cases, a reflection of social values.

This book was written to benefit sociology students, law enforcement officers, and anyone else in a position to be concerned with, or affected by, the issues of discrimination, persecution, criminal profiling, and that which has come to be referred to as racial profiling. Police administrators, judges, legislators, and business policy makers, must adequately understand the topics and their many practical, social, and legal ramifications if they are to make quality decisions that are based on fact rather than stereotype and myth, and free from the influence of adverse social and political pressures. And, attorneys, when prosecuting or defending cases wherein profiling and discrimination is an issue must have a good insight into the many interrelated dynamics of the topics to properly prepare and argue their case.

Accepting that anti-discrimination laws are intended to prevent unfair discrimination based on race, religion, color, sex, national origin, age, and disability, but also accepting that unfair discrimination is not limited to only those classes, it is clear that cultural awareness is prerequisite to understanding many aspects of the issues of profiling and discrimination and this book has been prepared accordingly.

An understanding of profiling and discrimination requires being able to view the issues within a social context that acknowledges the values and practices of the dominant society, as well as peripheral cultures, and relative to constitutionally protected rights. Hence, profiling and discrimination are not issues that can adequately be examined and understood in isolation, but are issues that are woven into the complex and ever changing fabric of society. And, while discrimination and persecution is generally contemplated relative to legally protected classes, an examination of the issues must, as stated, acknowledge that non-protected classes are also subjected to unfair discrimination.

Everyone has seen signs posted in business establishments stating, "We reserve the right to refuse service to anyone." It would seem that the right to discriminate, irrespective of protected or non-protected status, should be questioned relative to morals and constitutionally protected rights. There are many who feel that no licensed business, open to the public, should be at liberty to arbitrarily discriminate against anyone. So, while this book acknowledges discrimination against protected classes, it also acknowledges that members of non-protected classes are also subjected to unfair discrimination, even though such discrimination is legal. But, should it be legal? One must question, if police officers must have reasonable suspicion or probable cause to justify an investigative stop, irrespective of the subjects status whether protected or not, why then should businesses be at liberty to arbitrarily discriminate against those who do not belong to a protected class? For example, police must have reasonable suspicion or probable cause to legally subject a biker or a homeless person to an investigative stop, but the restaurant down the street may legally refuse such people service, and the motel owner is at liberty to turn them away. There is an apparent contradiction when citizens are protected against government abuses, irrespective of protected or non-protected status, but that same government leaves it legal for business owners to arbitrarily discriminate. On this issue, each reader is left to form his or her own opinion.

This writing is not intended to exonerate or condemn. It is intended to explore pertinent issues, provide insight, and provoke thought. An effort is made to offer views from different perspectives, often opposing views, of very socially complex and emotionally charged issues, but issues that are too often poorly understood and over simplified. And, when a real or perceived problem has been over simplified, the solutions that are implemented are too often themselves overly simplistic and do little more than give the illusion of having addressed a problem. That is especially likely when the issues are complex and controversial.

Discrimination relative to African-American's is addressed in this book but, additionally, two other groups have been selected for examination. That has been done because while they are both very prevalent in the United States, and subjected to considerable discrimination and persecution, little is understood about them. One group, bikers, is a multifaceted *subculture* and highly visible but not a protected class. The other group, Gypsies, is a *culture* that is uncharacteristically invisible or cryptic, and is a protected class.

Having selected those groups for examination will serve to broaden the reader's cultural awareness and sensitivity relative to profiling, discrimination, and persecution. And, as stated, it will illustrate the extent to which cultures and subcultures are often far more complex and enigmatic than realized. However, the book does not focus on them to the exclusion of other classes, and information is not provided about them that they would prefer be kept private. They are discussed, although superficially, for illustrative purposes because they feature some sociological uniqueness that would make their omission here unfortunate considering the scope and purpose of this book. Addressing them will leave the reader more aware of the diversity of cultures and subcultures and more insightful when considering the many other classes that are not discussed in this writing.

Difficulties of Political Correctness

A commonly heard term is *politically correct.* Being politically correct simply means that what a person says, and does, must be such that it offends no one improperly. Discussing profiling and discrimination, and the social context within which it occurs, is difficult without being at risk of being regarded by someone as being politically incorrect. Analyzing and discussing controversial and emotionally charged social issues such as these and remaining politically correct is difficult because not everyone agrees with everyone on various issues, and unfortunately the effort to remain politically correct can in many cases require sacrificing one's entitlement to free speech. No one agrees with everyone on such topics and even the two authors have differing views. That is to be expected considering that each is the product of a different environment and value programming process.

Most readers will agree with the authors on many points, but there will be points upon which they will disagree. That is to be expected. In fact, it is not the author's intention, or hope, that readers will embrace all the views reflected in this book. Rather, it is hoped that the reader will be left better able to explain why they agree or disagree on various issues.

Another element confounding the problem of analysis is the fact that the social sciences are not an exact science; they are fraught with ever changing variables. The social sciences feature a great deal that avails itself only to subjective analysis and interpretation rather than precise measurement. Hence, anyone analyzing social problems is influenced by their own frame of reference that has resulted from the manner in which they were socialized combined with the sum of their subsequent life experiences. Inherited traits can also factor into the equation. But, hopefully, each reader will examine what is said and be left with a better understanding.

Avoiding Errors in Logic and Reasoning

I know what I want to believe,
don't confuse me with facts!

Relative to the issue of discrimination and persecution, while a great deal has been accomplished in the United States, much remains to be done. However, if forward progress is to continue the issues must be addressed openly and candidly. If adverse social and political pressures result in those in policy-making positions skirting the issues to appease certain groups, forward progress will be impaired with one class likely being favored over another. Unfortunately, speaking out candidly, as necessary as it is, often puts the speaker at risk professionally.

Facts are stubborn and cannot be changed, and neither can history be changed. But, one can deny and misrepresent facts, and history can be subversively rewritten to conceal truth. When adverse social and political pressures result in distortions of reality, forward progress is impeded. When the former Colonel Carl Williams of the New Jersey

State Police made the controversial statement that Blacks and Hispanics were disproportionately represented in the trafficking of cocaine and marijuana, he was terminated by then Governor Christine Todd Whitman. It takes little imagination to understand how such an extreme response puts a chilling effect on others who will likely thereafter be more concerned with political correctness than with fact. When that occurs, debate will fail to reach a factual conclusion, and corrective measures will to varying degrees be errant. While facts may be unpleasant, they must be acknowledged and dealt with for what they are, for misdirected action can be worse than no action. A person once said, "If you don't want the truth, don't ask the question."

Debates regarding the issue of profiling, regardless of the level at which they occur, must focus on facts, however unpleasant. And, the emphasis must also be on feasible ways to ensure that racial bias does not pollute the legitimate practice of criminal profiling, and accomplish that in a way that does not impede the practice. Solutions must carefully avoid creating a situation whereby criminals realize immunity from arrest and prosecution, either because a law or policy grants immunity, or because a policy or law results in a chilling effect sufficient to deter officers/investigators from doing their job properly and diligently.

Recently, in a televised report it was indicated that in the United States the disease AIDS is again on the rise with the most notable increase being among male homosexuals. Among homosexuals, the most notable increase was said to be afflicting African-American's and Hispanic's.

The speaker, representing a health organization, was able to publicly acknowledge the statistics without suffering a social and political backlash. That raises the question why publicly acknowledging those statistics is acceptable but acknowledging race and nationality relative to crime statistics is not, even if reliable data supports the observation.

When arrest data suggests that certain minority races and nationalities are disproportionately involved in crime, one can argue that the data is flawed because police unfairly target those groups while placing less enforcement emphasis on non-minorities. However, such an argument is contradicted by hospital emergency room data revealing that certain races and nationalities are disproportionately suffering drug overdoses, and suffering injuries and deaths as a result of drug related violence. Hospital data tends to lend credibility to the arrest statistics of law enforcement, and validates the argument that law enforcement does not target minorities because of racial bias, but is placing emphasis on where crime occurs. ☛

It is unfortunate that some of the most vociferous people relative to the profiling issue appear to not understand the issue well, many appear to not want to understand it, and some appear to have a secondary self-serving motive. Anyone in a policy-making position would be prudent to approach the issue in a sober manner that is free from emotional undercurrents and adverse social and political pressures. If they don't, their efforts can do more harm than good for those they allegedly desire to protect, and certainly can be to the detriment of society as a whole. An axiom that has merit here is, "We admire the capable ambitious person, we can tolerate the capable lazy person, but God save us from the ambitious fool!"

Avoiding common errors in logic and reasoning is very important when making a critical analysis of any issue if the dynamics are to be understood. That is especially true relative to the social sciences, and especially so when confronting the complex and emotionally charged issues of profiling and discrimination. Everyone has witnessed someone being so emphatic about some issue, bringing to it so much emotional baggage, that they were incapable of viewing the issue objectively.

Many have heard the term, "I know what I want to believe, don't confuse me with facts!" Everyone has a set of biases that to varying degrees impedes the ability to view certain issues in a completely objective manner, and without being adversely influenced by various enduring labels, stereotypes, and myths. Bias, unless kept in check, will almost always impede critical thinking. Critical thinking is a quality everyone should strive to achieve, critical thinking being "A form of thinking characterized by a willingness to ask any question, no matter how difficult; to be open to any answer that is supported by reason and evidence; and to openly confront one's biases and prejudices when they get in the way" (Appelbaum, 1995).

When confronted with information in this book that to varying degrees conflicts with personal views, put those views in suspension until it is understood what is being said and the rationale underlying the assertion. Having done that, one will know what they are agreeing or disagreeing with, and why.

Chapter 2

CRIMINAL PROFILING
(Police Profiling Practices)

Generally speaking, it can be said that while the vary nature of profiling is discriminatory, it is not wrong when done for a legitimate purpose and it does not violate constitutionally protected rights. But, when profiling becomes the means, in whole or in part, to execute one or more acts of unfair discrimination, or persecution, it is wrong.

Q: What is a profile?

A: Profile can be defined as a short but descriptive biography describing the most outstanding characteristics of a subject.

Q: What is criminal profiling?

A: Criminal profiling can be defined many ways but, all definitions suggest a process whereby law enforcement personnel make judgments about another, relative to possible criminal activity, based on a number of overt and subtle factors which may or may not include such things as the person's race, national origin, manner of dress and grooming, behavioral characteristics, when and where the observation is made, the circumstances under which the observation is made, and relative to information the officer/investigator may already possess.

Q: What is racial profiling?

A: Racial profiling is a term that is generally understood to mean enforcement action on the part of police officers that is motivated more by racial bias than by any reasonable suspicion or probable cause that may exist under the circumstances.

Q: When race and/or national origin is included in a criminal profile, does the criminal profile become a racial profile?

A: No. Just because a criminal profile includes race or national origin does not mean it reflects racial bias or lends itself to discrimination or persecution; it's a question of relevancy. In fact, the racial issue is just one of many factors in the process of profiling someone and, often, when criminal profiling is being done race is not an issue at all. However, racial bias can pollute the legitimate practice of criminal profiling.

Introduction

Criminal profiling is a term used within the law enforcement community that refers to the art of crime detection wherein police officers are perceptive to various indicators suggesting that someone may be engaged in criminal activity. Criminal profiling is often confused with, and incorrectly thought to be synonymous with, the term racial profiling. The confusion results, at least in part, from a general misunderstanding of the practice of criminal profiling, and a natural aversion to what has come to be called racial profiling. Confusion has also resulted, in part, because a criminal profile will often include, among other things, race and/or national origin.

This chapter is not intended to teach the art of criminal profiling, but to clarify what it is to facilitate differentiating between criminal profiling and that which is referred to as racial profiling. While it can be argued that racial profiling is wrong, criminal profiling is both legitimate and necessary if law enforcement efforts are to be effective. And, just because a profile includes, among other things, race or national origin does not (should not) render it illegitimate. Minorities who are the subjects of criminal profiling, when criminal profiling is being properly done, do not capture law enforcement attention because they belong to a certain race or ethnic group, but because race or ethnic status has proven to be a relevant factor when considered in conjunction with other pertinent profiling criteria under the circumstances. And, there are criminal profiles wherein race and national origin is not considered because they are not pertinent factors in those instances.

Police officers assigned to various investigative departments use profiling techniques, out of necessity, to identify suspects relative to the types of crimes falling within their area of responsibility. Drug enforcement investigators have compiled lists of criteria, or in other words profiles, that suggests to them that someone may be involved in the transportation and/or selling of illicit drugs, or transporting drug money. Anti-gang units have compiled lists of criteria, profiles, suggesting that someone is or may be a street gang member. Similarly, U.S. Border Patrol agents have compiled lists of criteria, profiles, suggesting that someone may not be in the country legally, or may be transporting drugs or drug money. Serial killers, arsonists, and rapists, have also been profiled by the FBI's Serial Crime Unit to assist local investigators in the investigation of severe and/or serial crimes. The profiler, after examining all known elements of a crime(s), will construct a profile suggesting the type of person being sought. Such a profile enables investigators to be more focused in their investigative efforts.

While the members of various law enforcement units employ the use of profiles, the criteria that is meaningful to each is different, as would be expected. For example, the M.O., and therefore the profile, of a burglar will be different than that of a robber, or drug dealer.

The Origin of Criminal Profiling

It should be clear at this point that police in various areas of law enforcement have always utilized criminal profiling as an investigative tool, although it was not until recent times that the label of profiling was applied to the practice; police did it but there was no name for it.

Criminal profiling techniques have been in use since police first walked a beat. In England, in the time of the Georges, the detective was commonly called a Bow Street Runner, men of powerful physique, not always sophisticated but innately street-smart, and whose name and function reigned terror in the land. They were brutal! A parallel will be found when contemplating the sheriff in many early American communities, especially in the expanding West. Not uncommonly the inhabitants of such towns were victim to rogues who did as they pleased without accountability. The response was to employ the toughest rouge available and for perks more than paltry pay served to keep the townspeople safe from other rogues. As time passed, better hiring and training of police officers replaced that practice, yet an officer with advanced education was rare. However, that has changed. Today, police are increasingly sophisticated with increasing numbers having college degrees. While the Bow Street Runners almost certainly employed the practice of profiling, their need to profile effectively was likely diminished because of the liberal authority they enjoyed contrasted with the limited civil rights of the populous. Today's police officer must understand the various laws governing their conduct and profiling efforts must be measured accordingly.

Criminal profiling is possible because criminals tend to establish a modus operandi, or M.O. *Modus operandi,* a Latin term meaning a manner of operating, is defined by investigators as the distinctive features of the manner in which a criminal perpetrates his or her offenses, and it is the distinctive features that represent a pattern of criminal behavior resulting in what is referred to an M.O. Hence, an M.O. creates a profile reflecting a method of criminal behavior sufficiently distinctive that investigators are able to deduce that the same person or group committed two or more crimes. It is also M.O. that enables police to identify criminal suspects.

The first effort to systemize modus operandi data and render it useful to investigators was made by Major General Sir Llewelyn W. Atcherley, then chief constable of West Riding of Yorkshire, Wakefield, England, and culminated in the publication of "The Atcherley M.O. System", in 1913. The primary purpose of the M.O. system was twofold: (1) the identification of the unknown criminal before his arrest, and (2) subsequent to his arrest, the clearing of all crimes for which he was responsible. The first adaptation of the M.O. system in the United States was made under the direction of Chief August Vollmer of the Berkeley, California, police department. Chief Vollmer, in an article appearing in the *National Police Bulletin,* October 31, 1921, stated. "From old investigators, long experienced in the investigation of crime, we have learned that nearly all professional criminals have their specialty and seldom depart there from. For example, the robber does not stoop to commit burglary; the burglar believes that check passers are fools and take too many chances; while the check passer cannot understand why the robber risks life and liberty in a holdup when it is easier and less risky to obtain money by the use of wits and a worthless check. And so on through all the types of professional crooks. Not only do they specialize in particular crimes, but within the ranks of specialists we find differences in their mode of attack which are useful hints to careful investigators." People are creatures of habit and will utilize a given M.O. until circumstances require a change. But, even when M.O. changes are made, certain aspects of the M.O. will to varying degrees persist. It is M.O. that makes profiling possible.

Years ago investigators used the term portrait parlé. A portrait parlé is a word picture or, profile. And, while the portrait parlé placed great emphasis on the physical description of suspects, it also considered modus operandi. For example, if a burglar entered through a small opening and then used a chair to reach something, tall fat people would not be suspect for the perpetrator was obviously skinny and short. Such a deduction has its basis in the fact that a fat person could not have entered through the small opening, and it would not have been necessary for a tall person to stand on something to reach the desired object. Other evidence such as the type of premises burglarized, type of property stolen, type of burglary tool(s) used, and the time at which the crime occurred, adds to the profile. Such evidence results in a profile that enables investigators to become focused in their search for a suspect.

It should be clear at this point that police in various areas of law enforcement have always utilized criminal profiling as an investigative tool, although it was not until recent times that the label of profiling was applied to the practice; police did it but there was no name for it. However, law enforcement did use the term portrait parlé, which was a component of the Modus Operandi System. And, police did compile what they called rogues' galleries, which consisted of a compilation of photographs of known criminals in "mug books" which could be shown to crime victims in hopes they could identify the perpetrator. The term portrait parlé is obsolete, the Modus Operandi Systems have fallen into disuse, but rogues' galleries are still compiled by many police departments and will feature such criminals as sex offenders and gang members. However, the term rogues' gallery has fallen into disuse.

Profiles Are Both Static and Dynamic

*However, because criminals often change or modify their M.O. in an effort
to thwart law enforcement, profiles today are not as absolute and reliable as
they were in the past.*

Because an M.O. is a learned behavior, because circumstances
change over time, and because people are creatures of habit, an M.O.
will tend to feature both dynamic and static qualities. When something is found to work there is little incentive to change it until circumstances so require. But, even when an M.O. changes in response
to circumstances, certain aspects tend to go unchanged resulting in the
perpetrator leaving a signature, the signature being some specific fea-
ture(s) unique to the individuals M.O. that makes the crime distinctive
and recognizable as that person's work. Remember, people are creatures of habit.

Regarding the predictable nature of people, the reader may wish to
refer to one of the author's recent books that devotes considerable
attention to that issue, even to the extent of discussing how the environment often enables the astute investigator to make predictions
about someone, and how a person's domestic animals often provide
revealing clues about the owner. (Siljander: *PRIVATE INVESTIGA-
TION AND PROCESS SERVING: A Comprehensive Guide for
Investigators, Process Servers, and Attorneys.* Springfield, IL, Charles C
Thomas, 2001.)

When reading the section about the criminal profiles of drug couriers, the reader will observe that drug couriers utilize many different
methods to smuggle drugs and, accordingly, they are utilizing various
modus operandi. But, while each has an M.O. unique to themselves,
they all tend to exhibit an M.O. that has much in common with another and once law enforcement discovers what it is, investigative and
interdiction efforts are focused accordingly. For example, drugs smuggled across the United States/Mexico border are often concealed in
hidden compartments of cars, trucks, semi-trailers, boats, motor
homes, and other vehicles. Mexican citizens often drive these vehicles
loaded with drugs across the United States border through ports of
entry. But, because U. S. Customs agents may scrutinize Mexican citizens more closely than U.S. visitors returning to the states, drug dealers will often utilize senior citizens, college students, or other incon-

spicuous persons to smuggle the drugs across the borders due to their ability to pass through ports of entry with less scrutiny. That illustrates how drug dealers are dynamic and will modify their methods of drug smuggling, their M.O., in response to circumstances. But, as always, eventually the new method is discovered by law enforcement and drug or money shipments begin to be intercepted. Again, the M.O. will be modified. It's a cyclic situation.

Although methods of operation are dynamic and tend to change frequently in terms of specific M.O., the general dynamics tend to remain to varying degrees static. Accordingly, police officers have yielded numerous drugs and cash seizures, and effected countless arrests, by utilizing profiles that were developed in the 1980s. Hence, many traditional methods of drug couriers are still in use. However, because criminals often change or modify their M.O. in an effort to thwart law enforcement, profiles today are not as absolute and reliable as they were in the past.

The Origin of the Drug Courier Profile

Hence, who becomes the primary suspects will depend largely upon who is trafficking and the networks they cultivate. Naturally language and culture is an influencing factor.

The 1980s were the beginning of a major challenge for law enforcement because vehicle use for the interstate transportation of drugs and illicit money increased. Drugs that had traditionally been transported into Florida by air and water were now being smuggled into the U.S. through Mexico. Drug enforcement investigators, in an effort to identify couriers of drugs and/or illicit money, developed new profiles.

Relative to drug courier profiling, the age group with the highest rates of drug use, those falling within twenty to forty-five, were singled out. Persons displaying a style of dress that was considered flashy, or wearing an abundance of large gold jewelry, were also identified as fitting a profile. Many other indicators were also identified. Drug couriers were often sporting a couple days growth of facial hair, and displayed a general unkempt appearance, due to long road trips. The couriers traveled interstate highways, often at night, and in large vehicles capable of carrying greater quantities of drugs. Rental cars were commonly used so that the vehicle was mechanically reliable, and in the event of an arrest the vehicle was not subject to seizure for forfeiture.

Using traditional profiling techniques, ethnic minorities, usually Blacks, Hispanics, or other dark skinned subjects were singled out at higher percentages than persons of lighter skin because, at the time, they were considered to be the distributors of most major illicit drugs. The El Paso Intelligence Center (EPIC), the federal clearinghouse for drug-interdiction data, has validated reports that on a nationwide level, Blacks and Hispanics are represented at higher percentages than Whites amongst those arrested for trafficking in drugs. It is unclear, though, whether the imbalance is due to fair profiling practices or unfair racial discrimination. The imbalance could be the result of fair profiling if it is true that Mexican and South American Drug Cartels are well integrated with Hispanic communities in the U.S. This effect is evident in the Phoenix Metropolitan area where undocumented Mexican citizens maintain control over most of the marijuana, cocaine, and heroin, smuggled into the U.S. from Mexico.

To put the issue of singling out dark skinned people into perspective, relative to racial bias, one can compare that situation with the Golden Triangle of Myanmar (formerly Burma), Laos, and Thailand wherein it is Asians that are exporting heroin to the United States. Their distribution networks within the U.S. are predominantly Asian, which is to be expected. Relative to trade associated with the Golden Triangle, the profiling criteria would focus more on Asians than Hispano-Latino people. That is because those in the countries of origin will tend to utilize like ethnic gangs or distribution networks within the United States. Hence, who becomes the primary suspects will depend largely upon who is trafficking and the networks they cultivate. Naturally language and culture is an influencing factor.

Probable Cause, Reasonable Suspicion, Mere Hunch, and Intuition

It is not possible to say with certainty where the line is that separates mere hunch from reasonable suspicion; where does a hunch or intuition end and reasonable suspicion begin? While the line of distinction is often unclear, it would seem to relate back to the requirement that there be specific and articulable facts.

Before proceeding with this discussion of criminal profiling, an examination should be made relative to what constitutes probable cause, reasonable suspicion, mere hunch, and intuition. Humans are intuitive, some more than others, and people in certain occupations become highly intuitive relative to certain aspects of their job. Because police intuition is often a factor when considering reasonable suspicion and probable cause, and because intuition is also a factor when profiling, it would be worthwhile to examine those concepts.

Probable cause (reasonable cause) can be defined as a circumstance whereby one has more evidence for than against. Probable cause offers a reasonable basis for belief in certain assumed facts. Probable cause presents one or more probabilities that are based on factual and reasonable considerations that influence the deductions of a reasonable and prudent person and represent more than mere suspicion. But, probable cause offers less than the quantity or quality of evidence that will be required for a conviction in a court of law. *Reasonable suspicion* is that degree of suspicion that will justify a police officer in stoping a suspect in a public place, and is a quantity of quality of knowledge sufficient to justify a belief that criminal activity is afoot. Reasonable suspicion must be rooted in specific and articulable facts sufficient to support a rational inference relative to possible criminal activity, and be sufficient to justify an investigative stop relative to the constraints imposed by the Fourth Amendment.

In the above definition of reasonable suspicion was the term rational inferences. So, what is a rational inference? *Rational* can be defined as that which is based on sound principles of logic and reasoning. *Inference* can be defined as a logical conclusion or deduction based on pertinent information, while *intuition* is the awareness of something in the absence of conscious reasoning. A *hunch* may be defined as a suspicion or premonition thta something is about to happen but is not necessarily based on articulable facts.

When examining the various dictionary definitions, it becomes apparent that there is considerable overlap and that the concepts tend to work in concert rather than independently. But, while intuition and rational inference may suggest that someone is guilty (of something), before stopping the person can be considered justified, there must be "reasonable suspicion" or "probable cause" based on specific and articulable facts. It is not sufficient to simply say, "He looked guilty!"

Consider the case where a police officer on routine patrol observed two males in their early twenties walking away from a bar shortly after midnight. As they walked they were conversing and the officer immediately thought, "They are conspiring to do something illegal!" Accordingly, he turned at the next corner, circled the block, and reentered the area with the patrol car lights extinguished. Within a very short period of time the two individuals were observed running from between two houses, through a park, and down to a riverbank. One of the individuals was carrying something under his arm that the officer was unable to identify, but when first observed neither individual was carrying anything. At that point the officer had reasonable suspicion that a crime had been committed and radioed for backup while simultaneously flooding the suspects area with light. Immediately upon radioing for backup, a radio transmission was received reporting that a street robbery had just occurred in that area. The two individuals had robbed a waitress who had just gotten off work and was returning home on foot. The object the one individual had under his arm was subsequently determined to be her purse.

How did the officer know that the two men were going to commit a crime? He didn't! But his suspicions (intuitions) were sufficiently strong that he did not ignore the matter. People are intuitive to varying degrees but they are not psychic (most believe). Hence, in the absence of being psychic, there must be something that causes an intuitive person to sense something. In the case of the two robbers, when first observed it was their body language that suggested they were not engaged in casual conversation but, rather, were conspiring something. While conversing they would lean in the direction of each other and speak towards the other's ear in a manner uncharacteristic of two males engaged in casual conversation, the space between them was less than is generally the case when two males walk and talk, and they seemed too focused, so much so that they did not appear to even notice the passing squad car. Also, their age was a factor, as was the time, location, and direction of travel. Finally, one being a known criminal gave a greater degree of relevance to the observations. Did the suspicion justify stopping them? Certainly not for it had not yet reached the level of reasonable suspicion; it was still just a hunch. Was the officer justified in discretely observing the young men? Absolutely! Although the officer lacked the "probable cause" or even the "reasonable suspicion" necessary to justify making an investigative stop, his suspicions based on insight (intuition) resulting from his law enforcement training and experience coupled with a general understanding of human behavior justified discretely watching the two individuals until his suspicion was confirmed or dispelled.

In that example, what began as mere hunch escalated into reasonable suspicion when the two men were observed running in a headlong fashion from between two houses while carrying something that only moments before was not in their possession. Under the circumstances they appeared to be running from someone or something. At that point there was reasonable suspicion that a crime had been committed and pursuing them was justified, especially so once having received the radio transmission alerting officers that a robbery had just occurred in the area. When the two individuals were subsequently apprehended with the victim's purse in their possession, there was then probable cause to justify making an arrest and taking the two men into custody. Hence, what began as mere hunch turned into reasonable suspicion, and then escalated further to where there was probable cause.

It is not possible to say with certainty where the line is that separates mere hunch from reasonable suspicion; where does a hunch or intuition end and reasonable suspicion begin? While the line of distinction is often unclear, it would seem to relate back to the requirement that there be specific and articulable facts. Hence, each situation must be evaluated on the basis of the circumstances in that instance. In *Terry v. Ohio*, the Supreme Court held that police may conduct an investigative stop when there is reasonable (articulable) suspicion that criminal activity is afoot. And, they may conduct a frisk or pat down if specific and articulable facts are present that suggests a subject may be in possession of a weapon. An officer cannot, however, arbitrarily stop individuals and conduct a frisk utilizing "officer safety" as a reason.

Police have frequently questioned a Gypsy street entertainer because, as they say, "we don't know who you are and most people don't do what you are doing." Is his being detained and questioned legally defensible? While it may or may not be, it certainly is not justified simply because the officers don't know who he is and because what he is doing is atypical. In the absence of an ordinance requiring a permit to do what he is doing, there would seem to be no defensible basis for his being questioned. If the municipality requires a permit, then ascertaining that he has the required permit is justified. But, just because the officer does not know who he is, and just because he is doing something out-of-the-ordinary, does not justify the encounter. In the absence of specific and articulable facts that would induce an ordinarily prudent person under the circumstances to believe that criminal activity is at hand, there is no reasonable suspicion or probable cause to justify his being detained and questioned. Hence, his being detained and questioned would seem to be harassment (persecution) because he is "different."

Given what some might consider being a stereotypical Gypsy appearance, is that a case of criminal profiling or racial profiling? It is neither. In the absence of other pertinent factors that would justify the detainment, it is persecution. It would be difficult to argue convincingly that the act of standing on a street corner singing with a guitar suggests that criminal activity is at hand.

A police officer may stop and question a person when there is reasonable suspicion to believe that an offense has been committed, or is being committed. An arrest can be made when probable cause exists in a quantity, or of a nature, that justifies it. Clues giving rise to reasonable suspicion can be subtle, but their being subtle does not render them insignificant and without merit. An example that illustrates subtle clues is an experiment that was done with a U.S. Border Patrol agent on the U.S. and Mexico border. A White man with dark complexion and dark hair subtly glanced away (did not turn his head but diverted his eyes) from the agent, breaking eye contact. The fact that the breaking of eye contact caused the agent to become suspicious was subtle but very apparent. The agent responded by asking questions sufficient to satisfy himself that the person was a returning American citizen, not a Mexican National trying to slip unnoticed through the port of entry.

In another case, a biker went to a Mexico border town with a college coed who dressed for the day as a biker. Although she dressed the part, not being a biker she did not exhibit the persona of a biker. When returning to the U.S., while passing through the port of entry on foot, one agent nudged another and pointed to her, and they proceeded to question her sufficiently to ascertain that she was an American citizen. She was questioned quite apparently because she was trying to look like something she perceptibly was not. The biker himself was not questioned. The agent's intuitions gave them defensible reasonable suspicion to make inquiry. The average citizen would probably have perceived her to be a biker, but their experience based intuitions told them she was not.

Another example illustrating how something subtle can be a significant component of profiling criteria is the criteria used by members of a youth outreach program when going into the street near a university campus seeking to locate and assist teenage runaways who are homeless. While many of the runaway youth are often indistinguishable from other youth on the basis of clothing, hairstyle, etc., it is the deteriorated condition of their shoes that betrays their status as a homeless runaway.

Racial Profiling vs. Criminal Profiling

The older agents, because of experience, were better at profiling and less inclined to be influenced by stereotypes and myth.

When asking, what is racial profiling, it would be appropriate to leave out the word racial and question simply, what is profiling? The truth to that lies in the fact that the racial issue is just one of many factors in the process of profiling someone and, often, when criminal profiling is being done, race is not an issue at all.

As stated earlier, a *profile* can be defined as a short but descriptive biography describing the most outstanding characteristics of a subject. Accepting that definition, it becomes apparent that what is included in the profile of a specific person or group will vary considerably. For example, when a young man describes his new girlfriend to another person, he offers a description of her, or in other words a profile, describing her most notable characteristics. Psychologists have compiled profiles listing notable and outstanding characteristics or symptoms consistently displayed for various forms of mental illness, and it is the profile of symptoms that makes diagnosis possible. Police have compiled profiles reflecting notable characteristics of people who engage in various types of criminal activity.

For purposes of this examination, we will examine profiling relative to the issue of discrimination, persecution, and criminal profiles. Hence, for purposes of this analysis, it can be said that *profiling is a process whereby police officers make judgments about another, relative to possi-*

*ble criminal activity, based on a number of overt and subtle factors which may
or may not include such things as the person's race, manner of dress and grooming, behavioral characteristics, when and where the observation is made, the
circumstances under which the observation is made, and relative to information
the officer/investigator may already possess.*

Relative to profiles, it can be said that in order to qualify as a profile the list of factors must be both relevant and true. Hence, when a
person's race or cultural status is included in a criminal profile,
whether it should be permitted or proscribed will depend on the
degree to which relevancy can be shown. Reflect back to the earlier
mention of the term reasonable distinction. Hence, it's a case of relevancy and truth.

A biker was once detained at a U.S. Border Patrol checkpoint so that
the dog could sniff him and his motorcycle for illicit drugs. In that
case his subculture status relative to prevailing stereotypes and myth
was probably the primary reason for his detainment. In another case
the same biker was detained at the Canadian border, when reentering
the U.S., while they scrutinized his identity and checked the registration of his motorcycle. In that case his being a biker (subculture status) was the reason for his detainment, but bias and stereotypes were
not a factor. He was scrutinized because the agents had been alerted
by Canadian authorities that a criminal fugitive Canadian biker may
try to enter the United States and they were on the alert for him.

When a person is stopped by police, or treated differently by anyone else, solely on the basis of their racial status, or subculture status,
in the absence of other pertinent factors, they are not the subject of
profiling. Rather, they are the subject of discrimination and/or persecution, depending upon the circumstances. Hence, there is a difference between the legitimate law enforcement practice of criminal profiling, and the illegitimate practice of discrimination and persecution,
although prejudicial views can pollute the process of legitimate criminal profiling. Generally speaking, it can be said that while the very
nature of profiling is discriminatory, it is not wrong when done for a
legitimate purpose and it does not violate constitutionally protected
rights. But, when profiling becomes the means, in whole or in part, to
execute one or more acts of unfair discrimination, or persecution, it is
wrong.

When reasonable suspicion or probable cause exists, police may
legitimately detain a suspect. But, an unjustified detainment is not

always done with bad intentions, but sometimes results because the officer simply does not understand. For example, as previously stated, a U.S. Border Patrol agent detained a biker traveling cross-country until the dog sniffed him and his motorcycle for drugs. The agent who detained him was young and inexperienced. When not detained the biker was usually waved through by an older agent who had learned through experience who is really suspect and who is not. The older agents, because of experience, were better at profiling and less inclined to be influenced by stereotypes and myth. However, criminal profiling is an art that extends beyond an individual officer's own personal experience. The necessity for data supporting the validity of a profile will be found in the fact that while an officer may feel he or she has developed a valid criminal profile, it may be flawed because the officer's perception is inaccurate. An officer, just like everyone, is to varying degrees biased and that can cloud their judgment.

That same biker has had occasion to cross the border into Canada without being detained beyond the routine questions. During one such crossing he observed a young Canadian couple's vehicle being searched by Canadian authorities with a great deal of undeclared merchandise being inventoried. They had been in the U.S. and were returning to Canada. How did the Canadian border agent's know to search their vehicle? Their suspicion was probably the result of profiling. Factors that were likely considered when profiling them was (1) their age, (2) what they were wearing, (3) type of vehicle they were driving, (4) the time of day, (5) the day of week, (6) the time of the month, (7) where they were coming from, (8) where they were going, (9) their body language, (10) the fact that they were Canadian citizens, (11) how long they had been in the U.S., and (12) possibly any significant sales that had been advertised by merchants in the nearby American city and the duration of the sales. None of those factors in isolation would offer a basis upon which to suspect them of trying to bring undeclared merchandise into the country. However, several factors working together can create a profile that legitimately renders them suspect.

Often a fine line exists between what can be regarded as legitimate criminal profiling, and racial profiling or, more appropriately stated, discrimination and/or persecution. To illustrate the fine line of distinction that often exists, consider two similar scenarios. In the first scenario a police officer observes a Black man driving an expensive late model vehicle in a predominantly White neighborhood and becomes suspicious and questions the man. Is that a case of criminal profiling, or persecution? In the absence of other pertinent factors suggesting that criminal activity is at hand, it is not a case of criminal profiling, but persecution. The fact that the man is Black, driving an expensive vehicle, and in a white neighborhood, does not give rise to reasonable suspicion that crime is afoot. There is a difference between stereotypes and criminal profiles. As stated earlier, it's a question of relevancy and truth. There must be articulable facts to suggest that criminal activity is at hand.

In the second scenario a young White male is observed driving a late model BMW in a predominantly Black neighborhood. Does that represent a criminal profile? Depending on the circumstances it may. For example, if it is known by law enforcement that in the area there is a significant amount of drug activity in the form of street sales, or there is a persistent presence of prostitutes, or both, it may be concluded that the individual is seeking to purchase drugs and/or sex. But, the motorists mere presence, in the absence of indicators suggesting criminality, is not likely to be accepted by a court as constituting reasonable suspicion sufficient to justify an investigative stop. The individual being White, in a Black neighborhood, and driving an expensive vehicle, does not reasonably suggest that crime is at hand for he could be in the area for a legitimate reason (i.e., he may be a landlord, an insurance sales agent, a parole officer, or he may have family or friends residing in the area). Whether an investigative stop would be justified would of necessity consider a host of other factors such as the time of day, whether the vehicle was being driven in a circuitous route, the drivers demeanor, etc.

While criminal profiles often consider a suspects race, circumstances can result in an unpredictable judicial response. For example, a case that was heard by the 6th Circuit Court of Appeals, *U.S. v. Travis,* law enforcement officers acknowledged that they had considered the suspects race as a component of their criminal profiling criteria. In response to that, the court stated "The figures introduced by the agents clearly show that the agents chose to encounter African-Americans and Hispanics in numbers far in excess of what probability would predict. The justification offered by the agents is that they are not proceeding entirely on the basis of race. Rather, they proceed on intelligence, experience, and instinct. Since their intelligence information indicates that the Crips and the Bloods (predominately African-American gangs) are a large factor in the inter-city drug traffic and these gangs are primarily using African-Americans and Hispanic females as couriers, the agents select African-Americans and Hispanics for surveillance. . .. Police investigations, which have a disproportionate impact on minorities, are held not to offend the Constitution unless the targeting is based solely on race. Furthermore, even if a prima facie equal protection violation is established, effective drug interdiction is recognized as a compelling government interest that defeats the claim."

The courts decision in *U.S v. Travis* was in direct opposition with the decision of the New Jersey Supreme Court's ruling in *State v. Patterson*. The court stated that an individual's race couldn't be considered at all when conclusions are reached or assumed as to a profile suggesting criminal activity. In a similar case the Minnesota Court of Appeals ruled on the actions of an officer who had stopped a vehicle that was being driven by a White male. The stop was made at 2:15 A.M. in a neighborhood occupied predominately by African-Americans and known for prostitution activity. Prior to stopping the vehicle the officer ran a registration check and learned that the registered owner lived twenty miles away. The court ruled that "it is clear that the stop of the appellant, which only took place after his probable residence was ascertained, is premised on the belief that after midnight, Caucasian males from the suburbs are only in the Summit University area for no good, and no good is all the Summit University area has to offer."

Recently one of the authors attended a narcotics school taught by the United States Drug Enforcement Administration (DEA). A block of instruction was devoted to the issues surrounding racial profiling as it relates to drug enforcement efforts. The DEA has for years taught Police Officers and Drug Enforcement Detectives techniques for intercepting drug and currency shipments on the interstate highways of the United States. The DEA has named this highway interdiction program "Operation Pipeline." This program is reminiscent to what was taught in the 1980s relative to the structure of drug distribution cartels, and the methods of transportation. Many of these distribution organizations were predominately a certain ethnic group. As a result of the controversy surrounding drug courier profiles and racial profiling, however, the training has been modified so as to not create false stereotypes in the minds of police officers that implicate only specific

ethnic groups. The training has also been regionalized to instruct officers on the activities of organizations that are operating in their jurisdiction, minority based or otherwise. "Operation Pipeline" was developed not only to impact drug and currency smuggling, but to reduce
other crimes that are associated with drug smuggling, distribution, and
use. The Federal Bureau of Investigation (FBI) has reported that 48%
of all homicides, 60% of all assaults, and 80% of all property crimes in
the United States, can be directly attributed to drugs. In addition to
drug and currency seizures, officers are apprehending fugitives, locating missing children, and discovering other crimes unrelated to drugs.
The program has been very effective in spite of the controversy that
surrounds it.

The class attended by the author was in the Southwestern United
States, and thus the training was focused on organizations that operate
in that area. Arizona was discussed in detail due to its close proximity to Mexico, and the large amount of drug and currency seizures that
occur in the state. Arizona is a transshipment point for drugs smuggled from Mexico. Mexico contracts with countries in South America
such as Bolivia, Columbia, and Peru to hold drugs for shipment, and
to smuggle and utilize distribution networks established by Mexican
Cartels. Due to the ethnicity of the cartels, being Mexican, many of
the smugglers arrested or implicated in drug smuggling are of that ethnicity. That does not mean however that other ethnic drug smuggling
organizations are excluded from investigation.

Racial profiling has become an issue with the DEA just as it has with
other law enforcement agencies. A senior DEA agent/instructor who
was discussing racial profiling discussed a situation involving an
Arizona State Patrol officer working the I-40 highway in northern
Arizona. Many drug and money couriers utilize the I-40 Freeway to
smuggle drugs to eastern parts of the United States from Arizona. The
patrol officer was exceptionally skilled at profiling drug couriers, and
one of his profile stops resulted in a court case involving a Black
motorist who was, subsequent to the stop, arrested for possession of
narcotic drugs. The motorist's defense was that he was the victim of
racial profiling. The defense attorney subpoenaed traffic stop data
from the officer's employer, that being the Arizona Department of
Public Safety, but the department did not maintain records relative to
traffic stops. However, the county in which the officer patrolled conducted a study and discovered that minority motorists were stopped at

a disproportionately higher rate than that of white motorists. The defense attorney also discovered that the officer kept his own statistics on his traffic stops just in case he was ever accused of racial bias in his enforcement efforts. The logistics and methods of his data gathering is unknown by the author but, nonetheless, the data he gathered dispelled any appearance of any racial bias. In this case the data supported him, but sets a frightening precedent for other officers that may be challenged on the issue of racial bias in their traffic stops, but are unable to produce documents to dispute an allegation of bias. The senior DEA agent advised that law enforcement personnel engage in profiling based on criminal behavior, not race.

Profiling Applications

Some of the areas of law enforcement in which profiling is practiced include vehicle or pedestrian stops, illegal immigration, drug and money smuggling, gang enforcement, burglaries and robberies, and the investigation of serial crimes such as arson, rape, and murder. A brief summary of some such applications will be provided and, although the discussion is not exhaustive, it will provide an understanding of how and why profiling is utilized by law enforcement to aid in the detection and suppression of various types of criminal activity.

Profile Stops

A profile stop is only as valid as the indicators comprising the profile that underlies the reason for the stop. When considering a vehicle or pedestrian stop and detention, reasonable suspicion is the determining factor governing whether the stop will be accepted by a court as having been legitimate and therefore legal.

For example, in the event that a person runs or walks away from a police officer, certain elements are required to be present in order for the police to legally pursue and detain the individual. The officer cannot stop and detain a person simply because they chose to leave the area. Pertinent elements can include such things as whether the neighborhood is considered a high crime area, the time of day, or the fact that the suspect exhibits behavior that gives rise to reasonable suspicion that will meet the "reasonable officer" test. Relative to the area being a high crime area, the assertion must be supported by statistics, and not simply be the officers opinion. Also, the officer must be prepared to define what constitutes a high crime area. Some indicators that can provide reasonable suspicion include, but are by no means limited to, the following actions of a suspect:

1. Usually nervous.
2. Appears to be "casing" a location.
3. Conceals an unknown object.
4. Is looking around suspiciously.
5. Is wearing some type of disguise or clothing to obscure physical appearance.
6. Is at or near the scene of a crime.
7. Is conspicuously fleeing for an unknown reason.
8. For some articulable reason fits the profile of a criminal.
9. Abandons property for no apparent reason.
10. Is carrying what could be construed to be a burglary tool such as a large screwdriver or pry bar.

In most cases reasonable suspicion will not exist on the basis of only one or even a few of the above indicators. But, when a sufficient number of the above indicators are present, or when certain indicators are observed under appropriate circumstances, there can be a basis for reasonable suspicion. Hence, when considering the totality of the indicators along with the circumstances under which they are observed, there may or may not be a basis for reasonable suspicion. For example, the fact that someone runs from a police officer may not constitute reasonable suspicion. But, a person can become a suspect and be pursued by police if they run away in a high crime area, or if flight occurs at two o'clock in the morning.

In *Illinois v. Wardlow*, 120 S. Ct. 673 (2000), police officers were traveling through a high crime area when Wardlow saw them and ran. The officers pursued Wardlow and found an illegal handgun in his possession. The case was heard in the United States Supreme Court, and the court ruled that flight in a high crime area creates reasonable suspicion. Thus, the gun was admissible as evidence.

But, what if an individual who lives in a high crime area merely walks away from a police officer? In *Brown v. Texas* 443 U.S. 47 (1979), police officers approached two men in an alley that was known for drug dealing. The men saw the officers approaching and walked away in separate directions. The officers stopped one of the men, that man being Brown. The court ruled that, "the officers stopped Brown only on a mere hunch, and not reasonable suspicion. Law abiding persons live in high crime areas, and should not be detained based solely on that factor." The court ruled that, "a person should not be stopped simply because they desire to avoid contact with an officer by walking away from the officer, and live in a high crime area. Therefore a seizure of this type is unconstitutional."

In the first example (*Illinois v. Wardlow*) the suspect ran from officers, while in the second example (*Brown v. Texas*) the suspects simply walked away, and the court ruled differently in each case. The difference is a suspect in one case conspicuously running from police, while in the other case the suspects merely walked away. In *Terry v. Ohio* the Supreme Court ruled that "headlong flight" wherever it occurs, is the ultimate act of evasion and gives rise to reasonable suspicion that crime is afoot. However, the court did qualify its position by asserting that flight must still be evaluated relative to the totality of the circumstances under which it occurs. The Supreme Court stated: "Given the diversity and frequency of possible motivations for flight, it would be profoundly unwise to endorse a per se (bright-line) rule. The inference we can reasonably draw about the motivation for a person's flight, rather, will depend on a number of different circumstances. Factors such as the time of day, the number of people in the area, the character of the neighborhood, whether the officer was in uniform, the way the runner was dressed, the direction and speed of the flight, and whether the person's behavior was otherwise unusual might be relevant in specific cases." Hence, the Supreme Court was maintaining its "totality of the circumstances" approach to the issue of reasonable suspicion.

Drug Courier Profiles (Airport Interdiction)

What does a drug or money courier look like? Is there a profile that fits a traditional pattern of drug couriers? Investigators assigned to drug enforcement details utilize profiles to identify individuals and organizations involved in the use and/or distribution of illicit drugs. The various drugs have different but perceptible physical and psychological affects on a person, and the methods of distribution feature many indicators unique to the type of drug being distributed.

Drug courier profiles will differ in that some profiles will be relevant to dealers from drug source cities, and some will be relevant when considering money source cities. In the Southwestern United States, for example, drug investigators assigned to an airport are alert for profiles or indicators of persons arriving with money to purchase drugs, and persons flying out of the area with drugs. Most often the investigator will receive a tip (information) from an informant or investigator from a city that is the importer of illicit drugs. An investigator in Arizona, for example, may receive a tip that a person or persons in New York City purchased a twoday round trip airline ticket to Arizona with a money order on a holiday normally associated with heavy airline traffic. The ticket buyer appeared to be with a female who also purchased a ticket, but appeared to be trying to distance herself from the other passenger. Both tickets were purchased at the airport, and neither purchaser checked baggage. Both purchasers appeared to be nervous.

On the surface the information may appear insignificant, but significance can become apparent when analyzing the information against other factors. For example, the Arizona investigator will determine such things as whether a driver's license has been issued to those names, and if the persons have a criminal history. The race or national origin of the passengers may or may not be relevant depending upon the circumstances.

Law enforcement officers investigating drug or money smuggling to or from New York should familiarize themselves with Jamaican Posse organized crime methods of smuggling because they are a major participant, but not the only participant, in drugs being transported to New York. The Jamaican Posse is a criminal gang that originated from the ghetto areas of Kingston, Jamaica. From the late 1970s to a violent election in 1980, civil unrest forced many rebels to leave the country and flee to the United States with many settling in New York City. In the United States the gang members employed old gang alliances to form posses and began muscling their way into the cocaine trade. The gangs began to draw new members from those that had also fled Jamaica due to economic hardship. The illegal aliens were and are still used to provide security for stash houses, and loyalty is maintained by threatening the alien's family. Many in Jamaica revere the

Jamaican Posse members, viewing them as role models, because they often return to Jamaica wearing expensive jewelry and driving expensive cars (DEA).

Jamaican drug trafficking organizations operate in most areas of the country and purchase marijuana from Mexican sources along the Southwest border. Arizona, popular due to its close proximity to Mexico, is a location frequented by Jamaican drug smugglers for the purpose of procuring drugs for exportation to the East Coast, and to the Midwest. Because of close proximity, lower price, abundant supply, and ease, an estimated eighty percent of the United States supplies of drugs are smuggled through Mexico. The proceeds from drug sales are then smuggled back to the source area, and the profits are transported to Jamaica and possibly Europe.

Jamaican Posse groups use various methods and tactics when smuggling in an attempt to avoid detection by police. One Jamaican Posse group in particular often utilizes Jamaican women along with a White female to transport money and/or drugs. Typically, they use single mothers, often with children, and will utilize threats of violence to maintain control of the women. The women are generally dressed in business attire, and purchase airline tickets with a check or money order. They often purchase the tickets from different travel agencies and airlines, and travel on busy holidays and weekends.

As can be seen, drug couriers will often make an effort to avoid fitting a profile that is known to law enforcement but, in that effort, they often unwittingly create a new and unique profile. It is a bit reminiscent of the infamous U.S. criminal John Dillinger who used sandpaper to remove his fingerprints in an effort to render himself immune to identification via the science of fingerprints but, in the process, made his own fingerprints highly distinctive.

The investigator who incorrectly or disproportionately bases his or her courier profile on race or national origin, a Jamaican from New York City, for example, could be practicing what has come to be termed racial profiling. Although the investigator may be effective at intercepting drugs and money, and has discovered a profile that works for him or her, the case may not hold up in court if it is discovered that race or national origin was the dominant factor in the profile. More importantly, the investigator is probably missing a lot of good seizure opportunities because he or she is too narrowly defining who may be a suspect.

Case in point. An investigator learned during an interview of a Black suspect that he generally functioned as a decoy. Because he believed he would be the target of a drug courier profile stop, he would caravan with a white female who would drive a load vehicle (vehicle containing contraband) while he drove a second vehicle, a van. The hope was that law enforcement would target him while the load vehicle proceeded without scrutiny to its destination.

Drug distributors often use drug courier profiles to their benefit. Take for example a large Ecstasy distribution ring that was using the John F. Kennedy Airport as a main shipping point for Ecstasy pills being sent to the U.S. from Europe. The organization employed the use of decoy drug couriers to capture the attention of law enforcement while authentic drug couriers slipped by without scrutiny. That organization was fond of using single mothers with children, handicapped persons, and Hasidic Jews. The Hasidic Jews were paid approximately $1,500 to transport Ecstasy from Europe to New York City, but they were told they were smuggling diamonds and therefore did not know that they were trafficking Ecstasy. Additionally, they were paid an additional $200 finders fee for recruiting other Hasidic Jews to transport the "diamonds."

Because law enforcement began placing a greater emphasis on the seizure of Ecstasy entering the U.S. via airports on the East Coast, Ecstasy distributors have begun utilizing traditional distribution networks established by Mexican organized crime syndicates. That has resulted in large Ecstasy seizures in Mexico and in the United States along the Mexican border.

A Southwest United States investigator will utilize different profiling techniques to identify a drug or money courier. Taking the example of the ticket purchaser attempting to distance himself from the female ticket purchaser, one must look at the totality of the circumstances. If investigators are experienced in airport drug investigations and aware of the methods of smuggling money and drugs through airports, they will recognize indicators that fit the profile of a drug or money courier. Keep in mind that the indicators (profile) of a drug or money courier do not give the investigator probable cause, but often provide reasonable suspicion.

In *Sokolow v. United States*, 109 S. Ct. 1581 (1989), officers detained Sokolow who was exiting an airplane and asked for identification based on indicators suggesting that he fit the profile of a drug courier.

The indicators were that (1) Sokolow paid for the $2100 plane tickets with a roll of $20 bills, (2) he traveled under a name different than that listed for his telephone number, (3) his original destination was Miami (a major drug source city in the 1980s), (4) he stayed in Miami for only two days, (5) he appeared nervous, and (6) he did not check any luggage.

The United States Supreme Court ruled that each of the indicators, when considered in isolation, was indicative of innocent travel but, when all the factors were viewed together they created reasonable suspicion that a crime was being committed. All the factors, considered together, were consistent with what experience had demonstrated to be the profile of a drug and/or money courier.

When profiling drug couriers there can be a fine line separating what will be accepted by a court as having been a legal versus illegal detainment and/or arrest. Consider the case of *Reid v. Georgia*, 448 U.S. 438 (1980). In that case Reid fit the profile of a drug courier in several ways. He arrived from Fort Lauderdale, Florida, which was a major point of origin of cocaine trafficking in the 1980s, he arrived early in the morning when few law enforcement investigators were at the airport, he tried to conceal the fact that he was traveling with another passenger, and he had only shoulder bags. The officers stopped Reid and discovered drugs. The United States Supreme Court ruled that the profile did not create reasonable suspicion, and the evidence was suppressed.

Most cases of drug courier profiling must be examined on an individual basis because there are no well-defined rules as to what constitutes a defensible profile. The legality of most profiles will depend on various factors including the nature of the indicators, the number of indicators, the circumstances under which the indicators are observed, experience of the investigator, and comprehensive documentation of the profiling factors that were recognized and relied upon by the investigator.

When an investigator observes factors that he or she believes fit a drug or money courier profile, but is not sure if legally recognizable reasonable suspicion exists, the investigator may utilize a consensual approach and ask for permission to speak with the suspected courier. That is often the most prudent approach because by so doing the investigator can avoid executing a seizure that a court may later rule was made without reasonable suspicion and suppress the evidence on that basis.

Drug Courier Profiles (Vehicles)

Often, motorists will capture the attention of patrol officers for one or more reasons. Sometimes the reasons are obvious, and sometimes they are subtle. Police officers working the highways and city streets have learned that there are certain indicators that often suggest that a vehicle may be in the process of being utilized for the transporting of drugs. Naturally, the greater the number of indicators, the greater the likelihood that drugs or money is being transported. Officers relying on indicators that experience has demonstrated creates a reliable profile, must resist the tendency to begin concentrating solely on vehicles displaying such indicators while ignoring others because not all drug couriers will display the same indicators.

As was the case with drug couriers during the 1980s, rental cars are often utilized for drug transport, although personal vehicles are still used in over half the cases (Remsberge, 1995). Rental vehicles offer reliability against mechanical failure thus reducing the potential of an undesirable contact with law enforcement. Also, a breakdown requiring mechanical repairs increases the likelihood that the drugs or cash will be discovered in the vehicle while it is being serviced.

Rental Cars

Rental cars are used by organizations to distance themselves from the drugs or courier if the vehicle is stopped and the driver arrested, or the drugs or cash seized. For example, many organizations will park a vehicle at a location with drugs or cash hidden inside. A driver will be given a key to the vehicle that often will only operate the doors and ignition. Many times the driver of the vehicle will be told only to drive to a general destination and, once arriving, instructions will be provided as to where to park the vehicle and exchange it for another. The tactic, known as compartmentalization, is very effective in the event the driver is stopped by law enforcement inasmuch as the driver will not have access to the trunk and if consent is granted for a vehicle search, and the drugs are discovered, they claim no knowledge regarding the contents of the trunk and suggest that a previous renter must have left the drugs in the vehicle. Also, if police question the driver as to the drugs origin and/or destination, little information can be extracted from the courier who knows only from where the vehicle was picked up and the general area to which he or she was traveling. The vehicle is usually rented under a false name so that the identity of the renter is difficult to determine. Additionally, rental cars are not subject to seizure for forfeiture.

Many drug couriers don't know that they are transporting drugs, as was the case with the Hasidic Jews in New York City. Unwitting senior citizens are often paid a generous fee to transport motor homes across the country, often unaware that drugs or cash are secreted in the vehicle. But, sometimes they do know. Recently senior citizens have been arrested crossing the Mexican border into the United States smuggling drugs. When questioned, the senior citizens often report that the allure of receiving the motor home as payment for driving it across the border was too hard to resist. Even an elderly man in his eighties was arrested, and confessed to smuggling the drugs that were found in his vehicle.

Personal Vehicles

Personal vehicles used for transporting drugs offer couriers the ability to construct hidden compartments with the vehicles being used repeatedly to transport drugs and/or cash. That is reminiscent of the tanker cars used to transport illicit (bootleg) alcohol during prohibition. Often the vehicles will be purchased under false names to make it nearly impossible to identify the owner. The vehicle is often given as payment to the courier after the drug or cash shipment has been made. Temporary registration is often a very effective means of making it more difficult for law enforcement to determine the origin of the vehicle while in transit.

Vehicles originating from a drug source state, such as Arizona or California, observed in an eastern state along with other indicators, may become suspected of being a courier vehicle. Many couriers will carry license plates for each state through which they pass. Contradiction between indicators as to the state of origin of a vehicle can give rise to suspicion. For example, a vehicle featuring a dealer logo from one state while featuring a license plate from another may become suspect.

In Phoenix, Arizona, a Mexican drug organization utilizes V.I.N. switched vehicles with hidden compartments to transport drugs. In one case, a narcotics detective conducting surveillance of a drug house followed a vehicle from the house to a parking lot in a strip mall where a package was observed being transferred to another vehicle. The vehicle into which the package had been placed was subsequently followed and stopped for a traffic violation (pretext stop). Consent was granted to search the vehicle but nothing was found in the passenger compartment. A more thorough search resulted in the discovery of a hidden compartment in the shifter compartment of the center console. The driver was arrested and charged with possession and transportation of narcotic drugs for sale and the vehicle was seized for forfeiture. The vehicle was later found to be a V.I.N. switched stolen car. The Mexican organization was well aware of the benefit of utilizing stolen vehicles, hidden compartments, and vehicles registered to third persons.

As stated, vehicles utilized by drug couriers will often be modified to conceal drugs or currency, and they may display various indicators commonly associated with drug courier vehicles. The indicators of such vehicles are often subtle, but meaningful if one is aware of them. Drug courier vehicles may display the following indicators:

1. Rear end riding low (sagging under a load).
2. Spare tire or luggage in the back seat to make room for more drugs in the trunk.
3. Tinted windows, or windows down during unusually hot or cold weather.
4. Modifications or alterations to vehicle.
5. Very little luggage, if any at all (out of state vehicles).
6. Good guy decals such as religious symbols, pro-police stickers, or anti-drug stickers.
7. Lifestyle statements such as drug paraphernalia, decals of drugs, or decals of rock groups such as the grateful dead.
8. Multiple deodorants used to mask odors of drugs.
9. Dirty vehicle with clean plates, and/or clean tail light lens.
10. Clean vehicle with dirty plates.
11. Unusual driving such as driving slow or weaving, or perfect driving.

When considering the above indicators one should keep in mind that courts have generally held that stopping a vehicle solely because the vehicle fits a drug courier profile is unconstitutional because the vehicle of many innocent travelers will display such indicators.

Criminal/Street Gang Profiling

Due to the mobility of gangs, the following facts may change, as gangs are also dynamic in nature, not static. A street gang and its membership tend to result in a distinct subculture. Gangs tend to be distinguishable one from another by virtue of their agenda, style of dress, hand signs, slang speech, writings and graffiti, all of which identify a specific gang and its members. The symbols and signs are used to communicate the individuals gang affiliation to other persons whether gang members or not. The profile of a gang member is often difficult to establish because of changing clothing trends, norms, and the number of new gangs that emerge with rules and styles that often don't conform to traditional street gangs.

Most street gang membership consists of youth. The evolution of street gangs, the identifiers for individual gangs, and the motivators of young people to join a gang will not be discussed, although an overview of how gangs and their membership tend to fit a certain, but loosely defined, profile will be discussed relative to the topic of profiling.

The profile of a gang member will usually depend on the gang's motivations (i.e., selling drugs, extortion). When analyzing street gang membership as a whole, however, a disproportionate number of the following indicators are evident and may apply:

1. Usually male.
2. A school dropout or one that does not adapt well to school.
3. Has inadequate family affiliation.
4. Is a victim of parental neglect and/or abuse.
5. Comes from a lower or middle socioeconomic level.
6. Have negative role models.
7. Is very street smart, hostile, aggressive, and anti-social.
8. Tends to come from a home with no father figure, or a dysfunctional father figure.
9. While a certain percentage of American citizens suffer a learning disability in one form or another, a significantly greater number of those who are incarcerated suffer a learning disability, and so it is with gang members.

Physical attributes of a gang member commonly consist of indicators including but not limited to:

1. The wearing of certain colors (symbols or insignia) or clothing that is indicative of a certain gang. That can include matching clothes such as shirts, pants, shoes, caps, hats and bandanas. Colors are often an integral part of gang identification and often serve to promote group unity.
2. Graffiti written on articles of clothing, documents, books, bags and buildings and fences. Graffiti is one of the first indicators of gang activity in an area inasmuch as graffiti is used to mark territorial boundaries often serving as a warning and sometimes a challenge to rival gangs. Graffiti is designed to glorify the gang and make their existence well known.
3. Tattoos are commonly used to identify membership with a particular gang, chapter (set), and nickname (moniker). Tattoos appear anywhere on the members body and often are crude as they are generally done unprofessionally.
4. Hand signals, commonly referred to as gang signs, are used mainly as a means of communicating between allied and rival gang members. Hand signals are also used as a means of challenging rival gangs. Members can often be seen throwing signs (non-verbal communication), which is now illegal in many states.

When examining the factors that place a youth at high risk of becoming a gang member, and simultaneously examining the outward characteristics commonly associated with gang membership, a profile becomes apparent. But, specific profiles of gangs and their members will be largely dependent on certain factors such as the ethnic base of the gang (e.g., Black, White, Mexican, Asian), the type of gang (e.g., street, white supremist, outlaw bikers), and the region in which the gang is located.

Profiling to Locate a Suspect

While profiling is commonly done to identify those who are engaged in criminal activity, profiling can also be done when attempting to locate a suspect immediately following an offense. For example, one officer working uniformed patrol realized about a fifty percent success rate locating hit and run drivers subsequent to early morning automobile accidents, and he accomplished that by profiling. He would obtain, from the driver who remained at the accident scene, as complete a description as possible of the other driver and their vehicle. Then, based on the subject and vehicle description, coupled with the subject's direction of travel, and the time of day, he was able to be very focused in his efforts to locate the other vehicle. That was possible because he was able to deduce where such a person may have been going, the type of destination, as suggested by the profile. Some profiles suggested a college student, construction worker, office worker, restaurant worker, etc. He would check all possible destinations looking for a vehicle fitting the description, a vehicle also reflecting appropriate body damage and paint residue consistent with the other vehicle. The driver's physical description was also relevant once the vehicle had been located, and the driver then sought. Naturally, once locating a suspect vehicle a registration check would be made to determine ownership, and a check would be made for drivers license information under the registered owner's name. The officer worked in a small college town so his method was effective. Although such an effort would not be as successful in a large metropolitan area, those working such areas should not dismiss the rationale underlying that application of profiling.

Pretext Stops Relative to the Fourth and Fourteenth Amendments

Pretext stops do not violate the Fourth Amendment even if made for purpose of harassment. However, a pretext stop made for such a reason can be a violation of the Fourteenth Amendment.

Earlier, mention was made regarding pretext stops. In many situations when a police officer has become suspicious, but lacks the reasonable suspicion or probable cause necessary to justify making a stop, he or she will make what is called a pretext stop. A pretext stop is the stopping of a suspect for a legally justifiable reason, such as a traffic violation, burned out tail light, cracked windshield, etc., with the real intention for the stop being the officer's initial suspicion of possible crime that did not in itself justify the stop. This is where the opponents to profiling argue that police abuse the practice of pretext stops.

For those who may be tempted to consider pretext stops to be unjustified, consider it from the perspective that if such stops were ruled to be illegal, such a ruling could have the effect of requiring police officers to ignore violations of law that are observed subsequent to their becoming suspicious. This is not to imply, however, that the practice of making pretext stops cannot be abused for purposes of racial bias. That concern causes one to visit the issue of quality selection, training, and supervision, of police officers.

Despite the constitutionality of the practice of making pretext stops, motorists are often aware that they were stopped for a frivolous traffic violation so the officer could conduct a further investigation relative to his or her suspected criminal activities. This often creates anger towards law enforcement. This anger is often shared with the motorist's friends and family. Thus anecdotal stories circulate about the practice of police officers stopping minority motorists for minor traffic violations with an ulterior motive such as being in search of illegally possessed weapons or contraband. The unfortunate equation in all of this is that it may create an environment were police administrators become more concerned about their public image and may regard community relations as more important than arresting drug users or dealers (Hansen, 2000).

Pretext stops do not violate the Fourth Amendment even if made for purpose of harassment. However, a pretext stop made for such a reason can be a violation of the Fourteenth Amendment. The Fourteenth Amendment has to do with equal protection under the law. For example, a stop that is made without reasonable suspicion or probable cause, and therefore is without legal basis, is a violation of the Fourth Amendment. Conversely, a pretext stop that is allegedly based on a legitimate violation such as a burned out tail light, but is really for the purpose of harassing (persecuting) the motorist, is a violation of the Equal Protection Clause of the Fourteenth Amendment. While Fourteenth Amendment violations occur, proof is exceedingly difficult. Thus was the case of *Whren v. U.S.* where the United States Supreme Court ruled that the use of pretext stops were constitutional. The court, however, left open the possibility of attacking racially biased law enforcement activity under the Equal Protection Clause with civil suits. There are a number of suits around the United States pending or recently concluding, including those in Maryland, Florida, Iowa, and Illinois (Aether Systems', 2001). Refer to "Selective Prosecution of Minorities (Case Study)" in Chapter 3, "Fair Treatment Policies and Equal Protection."

The Unpredictability of Judicial Responses to Profiling

The ruling in that case acknowledged that race and nationality can be a legitimate factor when profiling if it can be shown to be relevant.

Earlier discussion emphasized that a fine line often exists relative to the distinction between legitimate criminal profiling and discrimination and/or persecution. That being the case, it is understandable why it is often difficult to predict how a court will rule when criminal profiling has occurred and is later challenged by the defense. For example, an airport detention, which led to an arrest, was made of a person who investigators stated fit the profile of a money courier. The person arrested was Black, dressed flamboyantly, and wore an abundance of heavy gold jewelry. At the time of his arrest, the defendant's appearance as well as other factors led investigators to believe he was a money courier. Prior to trial the defense attorney, who was White, dressed in a near identical fashion, including the heavy gold jewelry, and loitered about the airport for several hours without being questioned. The defense argument that ensued was that with all things having been equal, except for race, the fact that the White person (the attorney) was not questioned proved that the defendant had been detained because he was Black, not because of the other profiling criteria that had been applied. However, that was an invalid exercise for several reasons.

For the exercise to have been valid it would also have been necessary to have a Black person, dressed the same, loiter about the airport. But, with the exercise as it was, failure of the White attorney to be questioned may not have been because he was White, but because he did not satisfy any of the pertinent profile criteria that his client had satisfied other than to dress like him which, significantly, was not characteristic of a White person's dress and therefore could be argued to have failed to provide reasonable suspicion even on that basis. He did nothing to mimic the conduct and movements of his client except to dress like him. He had not purchased a ticket in the same fashion as the defendant and in fact had purchased no ticket, he had not arrived from the same place and in fact was not an arriving passenger, he did not have an apparent destination and in fact had no departure ticket, he had no carry-on or check-in luggage, and he was not seen with someone else suggesting an accomplice. All things considered, he did not satisfy any of the drug courier profiling criteria except to dress like his client and loiter about the airport for no apparent reason. Hence, he gave investigators no reason or justification to question him, although logic would suggest the possibility that he was being discretely watched to see what he may do, and whom he may meet.

In the final analysis, that exercise did nothing to substantiate that the defendant had been detained solely because he was Black. All it did was cloud the issue to create confusion between the legitimate law enforcement practice of criminal profiling and that which has come to be called racial profiling, and it was obviously successful in that endeavor since the judge ruled in favor of the defendant in a suppression of evidence hearing.

Examining the exercise from another perspective, one could argue that failure of investigators to question the attorney actually substantiated that investigators were working with complete criminal profiling criteria and not detaining people on the basis of insufficient indicators or mere hunch. Further, that Black people (apparently) who did not satisfy the other profiling criteria were not detained and questioned weakens the assertion that the defendant had been detained exclusively because he was Black, but was detained on the basis of pertinent profiling criteria.

Another case illustrating the difficulty of predicting how a court will rule relative to profiling is a situation that occurred in Arizona. In that situation, *State v. Graciano*, 134 ARIZ. 35. 653P. 2d 683, pickup trucks were being stolen from the Phoenix area and taken into Mexico. The trucks being stolen were very specific in terms of make, model, and year. They were being stolen from business parking lots (employee parking) during the week (Monday through Friday) by Mexican Nationals, and taken early in the day so that by the time the vehicle owner got off work in the afternoon, and discovered the theft, the vehicle had already been taken across the border into Mexico. Meantime, if a suspicious police officer ran a check on the license plate number, the vehicle would not reflect having been stolen because the owner had not yet discovered the theft. Nogales is little more than three hours from Phoenix and generally the vehicles were never recovered once having been taken into Mexico.

The Arizona Highway Patrol learned that when pickup trucks of a certain make, model, and year, were being driven by someone of Mexican extraction towards Mexico along I-10 between Phoenix and

Tucson, and on I-19 between Tucson and Nogales, at certain times of the day or week, there was a high probability that the vehicle was stolen. They began stopping such vehicles if they were south of Casa Grande which is about 60 miles south of Phoenix along I-10, and found that approximately nine of every ten trucks stopped were in fact stolen.

The police were accomplishing that admirable success rate by criminal profiling. The profiling criteria consisted of (1) make and model, (2) model year, (3) the highway upon which the trucks were being driven, (4) the direction of travel, (5) the time of day (early), (6) the day of week (Monday through Friday), (7) their being driven by a person of Mexican extraction, and (8) the observation being made south of Casa Grande. Vehicles of a different make, model, and year, were not stopped even if being driven by someone of Mexican extraction. Vehicles of the same make, model, and year, were not stopped if driven by someone other than Mexican extraction

The driver being of Mexican extraction was a relevant part of the profile, but it was only one of no less than eight factors as outlined above, and it was in no way rooted in racial bias. Ethnicity was every bit as relevant as the other profile criteria and, in fact, it was so important that if the driver was not of Mexican extraction, all the other profiling criteria became invalid. Hence, the vehicle was not stopped because someone of Mexican extraction was driving it, but because the person being of Mexican extraction was relevant when considered along with the seven other profiling criteria. As stated, if the driver was not of Mexican extraction, all the other profiling criteria became invalid and therefore were not acted upon.

Eventually a case found its way to the Supreme Court and a conviction was overturned. In that case the officer testified that, as he met the southbound vehicle, a clear view of the driver had not been possible and, therefore, when the decision was made to stop the vehicle the officer was uncertain as to the driver's gender, approximate age, and race. But, if such a determination had been made in that instance, would that have been a case of racial profiling? Would the constitutional rights of the driver have been violated? For purposes of analysis, relative to this example, consider this scenario. Two identical trucks are observed under identical circumstances, one is being driven by a White person and the other is being driven by a Mexican. The truck being driven by the Mexican person is stopped. Would that constitute racial profiling (racial bias)? Should the stop be declared unconstitutional? It could be argued that such a stop is not made because the driver is Mexican, but because the driver being Mexican is pertinent relative to the other profiling factors.

The ruling in that case acknowledged that race and nationality could be a legitimate factor when profiling if it can be shown to be relevant. To rule otherwise would have had the effect of creating a situation whereby police officers cannot use a person's race or national origin as part of a list of profiling criteria, even when it has proven to be relevant. It could create a situation whereby police are required to ignore what all things suggest may be a crime in progress, but a person's race or national origin grants them immunity. It could create a situation whereby that which is intended to protect a citizen's constitutional right could be argued to grant immunity to members of a protected class and, more specifically, the criminals among them.

Relative to the example here, proscribing race and/or nationality as a profiling factor would have resulted in trucks thereafter being stolen with immunity by requiring officers who have reason to believe a vehicle is stolen to simply permit it to continue into Mexico, or make a pretext stop (discussed previously), or stop the vehicle alleging probable cause even though none may exist beyond the profiling criteria that can no longer be applied. Under such circumstances which would officers do? Predictably, any of the above could occur. But, under such circumstances, if pretext stops increased, the argument could be advanced that racial bias had polluted the legitimate practice of making pretext stops, asserting that stops were being made on the basis of ethnicity. From what has been discussed here it can be seen how a ruling intended to protect can be detrimental if the larger perspective is not acknowledged.

Chapter 3

FAIR TREATMENT POLICIES
AND EQUAL PROTECTION

Anti-discrimination efforts can be no better than the caliber of the officers that are hired, the quality of the training they are provided, and the quality of management and supervision. And, of course, departmental policies must be well conceived.

Introduction

When various forms of discrimination and persecution can be proven to occur, and bias on the part of some police officers can be proven to occur, preventive measures must be implemented. But, how to solve such a problem without creating more serious problems becomes a practical concern with no simple solution. And, before embarking on an effort to solve a problem, the nature and extent of the problem must first be ascertained. Any competent administrator will acknowledge that before something administratively worthwhile can be done, one must first identify their objectives. It all relates back to the basic risk management framework of (1) problem identification and analysis, (2) treatment technique selection, (3) clarifying the method for implementation of the chosen technique(s), and (4) determining how results will be monitored. Hence, the issue to be addressed must be clearly understood and the plan to address the issue must be well conceived; what is to be done, how will it be done, who will do it, by when, and how will the results be monitored? This problem has a solution: competent legal training and oversight (Hansen, 2000). Relative to the issue of improper profiling by police, there usually is no need to embark on a systematic statistical data acquisition

51

project to determine the extent and nature of a problem, and usually a large-scale problem does not exist. Naturally, a wide spread problem, if it exists, will require a different response than will be necessary with problems that are sporadic, the latter more often being the case.

We live in an increasingly complex and ethnically diverse society and the issue of fair treatment of all classes cannot be ignored. But, any efforts intended to ensure fair treatment must be made cautiously and with full regard for practicality and possible adverse consequences. For example, there are many who feel that there is no effective way to reliably monitor police contacts relative to class such as race and national origin, but there are many problems that can result from such an effort. That will be discussed. Perhaps, instead of placing emphasis on the gathering of statistical data relative to police/citizen contacts, an effort that cannot as a practical matter result in reliable data because of the infinite number of ever changing variables, the emphasis should be on well conceived and unambiguous departmental policies, recruitment of high caliber officers, quality training that is ongoing and documented, quality supervision, and on a well trained and adequately funded Internal Affairs department. One must not lose sight of the fact that almost all police officers are honest citizens doing the best job they can, and if provided quality training their performance will reflect that training.

Regardless of what is done in response to a racial related problem, it is important to understand that the frustration level of minorities who feel the police have mistreated them runs high and generally they feel they have no recourse. Often, the perceived lack of recourse generates more frustration than the event underlying the grievance whether real or imagined. And, when discrimination is perceived to occur more than incidentally, it tends to generate fear of future discrimination. It is a sad fact that members of ethnic and cultural minorities do face discrimination and persecution in many forms, aside from job and housing discrimination, such as by being told to leave a shopping mall, restaurant, bar, church, or a town, because their kind is not welcome there. Many avoid certain parts of town knowing (or fearing) that their presence there puts them at high risk of being stopped by police, and in many cases entire towns are avoided. Many avoid traveling certain streets, especially at certain times of the day, or certain days of the week, for the same reason. Many fear having false charges levied against them supported by planted evidence and perjurious testimony knowing that such things do occur, even though such incidents are sporadic. Many have been reported for alleged code and zoning violations with the allegation based solely on speculation, or intent to harass, because they were not wanted in the neighborhood. The list could continue. A college instructor of a Police Administration course, the former chief of police of a major American city, frequently stated that people fear the power that police have. In reality, especially with minorities, it is not police power that frightens people so much as it is the potential misuse of that power. Minorities, much more than non-minorities, view with fear such things as selective enforcement, malicious prosecution, biased court decisions, police harassment, police brutality, selective code and zoning enforcement, repressive legislation, and failure of the police to respond or investigate when they have been a crime victim or, more generally, failure of the government to enforce laws that serve to protect them.

Many people believe that minorities and members of subculture groups are anti law enforcement when in fact they are more often simply anti police and governmental corruption. It would be accurate to say that many do not trust the police even though knowing that most (almost all) are in good faith trying to fairly serve their community; the few bad one's terrify them and they can't tell the good from the bad. The person who has not experienced discrimination and persecution in its varied forms cannot view it, and fear it, in the same manner as those who have. And, discrimination is more pervasive in American society than many White middle class people tend to realize. The White middle class person, when stopped by police, expects to be treated with some degree of courtesy while the minority or member of a subculture group tends to fear treatment that is less than courteous. This writer recalls seeing a large sign painted on the side of a building in a Black neighborhood that read: "Stop Police Brutality! How do you call the cops on the cops?" True, police departments have an Internal Affairs Division, and their investigations are usually unbiased, but it is vitally important that those who feel they have a valid complaint believe Internal Affairs is unbiased. Adverse reactions are more likely when someone believes they have been mistreated, but they also believe they have no recourse through legitimate channels. Internal investigations can identify officers involved in misconduct and the situation can be resolved by appropriate remedial training, discipline such as written reprimands, days off, and in extreme cases, termination. Those are an immediate and effective remedy to a problem.

Those who are assigned to the Internal Affairs Division are in a difficult position. They must diligently investigate complaints and do so in a manner that leaves the complainant feeling that they are sincere in their efforts, yet do their job in a way that does not appear to be the proverbial "witch-hunt." Overzealousness on the part of Internal Affairs can create a chilling effect that detrimentally impacts the efficiency of the officers being investigated, as well as all other officers. No one benefits if officers feel they are in a no win situation; "I'm damned if I do, and damned if I don't." When police officers become less concerned about enforcing laws, and more concerned with staying out of the way of Internal Affairs, the citizens suffer. If anyone needs and wants the benefit of quality law enforcement it is the many very good but unfortunate people, economically poor, many of who are minorities, living in blighted crime ridden neighborhoods. It is unfortunate when the vociferous few, who falsely claim discrimination, and those who yield to their unfounded claims in an effort to pacify them, diminish the protection to which the citizens are entitled.

The Difficulty of Monitoring Fair Treatment Policies

They will favor one class while penalizing another so that scrutiny will not suggest bias even though it has become a fact, in response to the scrutiny.

One practice intended to prevent and detect bias on the part of police officers is to track how many traffic stops are made, citations written, and arrests made, relative to different classes. That is done to determine if police officers are disproportionately stopping, citing or arresting the members of certain classes because of bias. On the surface it would seem that there should be an even distribution, or at least a distribution that is consistent with the racial/ethnic composition of the community in question. But, for there to be a correlation it must be assumed that the members of each class commit an equal number of offenses. An equal distribution is almost never the case and will vary by area. Some White neighborhoods have a higher crime rate than other White neighborhoods, and so it is with areas inhabited disproportionately by Blacks, Asians, Mexicans, etc. And, what is the nationality composition of a "White" neighborhood? Many who are generally considered to be White embrace a strong cultural identity, retain ties to those in the old country, and continue to cluster into ethnic communities even though others in the community are unaware of their clustered presence.

A Black police officer patrolling a predominantly White community will issue far more traffic citations to White people than he or she will issue to Black people. And arrests for crime will more frequently involve White people. Similarly, a White police officer patrolling a predominantly minority community will cite and arrest far more minorities than White people. That fact does not make them guilty of racial bias. And, if the ratio of traffic citations and criminal arrests relative to ethnic class are going to be tracked, not only should the racial demographics of the area under scrutiny be considered, but also the racial mix of the officers assigned to that area. Monitoring such a situation is difficult, if not impossible, because of the numerous variables involved. For example, if one White police officer, and one minority police officer, were assigned to patrol a given community, one may cite and arrest more members of the class therein because he or she intuitively better understands the cultural dynamics of the class in question which leaves them more astute in their enforcement efforts. The list of potential variables could continue to near infinity. Also, it must be remembered that in the United States there are an estimated 88 different cultures and languages and monitoring efforts will tend to focus on a few while ignoring others.

One of the most predictable responses by police officers, when their performance relative to bias is being scrutinized, is to begin issuing fewer citations to all classes as a form of protest, or begin citing fewer minorities while (possibly) increasing the number of citations being issued to White people so as to skew the numbers in a manner sufficient to avoid having to explain themselves. Officers may begin issuing "borderline" tickets to Whites while overlooking infractions when committed by minorities. Assuming that officers were being fair and impartial in the citations that were originally being issued, and in the arrests that were being made, logic suggests that their response results in their no longer being fair and impartial. They will favor one class while penalizing another so that scrutiny will not suggest bias, even though it has become a fact in response to the scrutiny. Most people have heard the term "reverse discrimination," and that serves as one example of it. But, relative to the issue of reverse discrimination, there is basis upon which to debate if there really is such a thing, or if it is simply a term that raises the question of whether someone is being discriminated against in favor of someone else, and why.

Prevention is difficult to measure, yet studies have shown that when police enforcement efforts are relaxed, offenses increase proportionately. If that occurs, the honest majority of the favored class will suffer increased offenses in their community. If that occurs, it can be argued that favoritism has hurt rather than helped a class of people, their community as a whole. Most minorities, like the people of any other class, are honest citizens. And, they are not anti-law enforcement as commonly believed (by White people) but, rather, they are anti police and government corruption. When pressure from a vociferous few results in relaxed enforcement efforts within a community, the honest members of that community are made to suffer unfairly and unnecessarily.

When internal policies, court rulings, and legislative actions, create a situation that puts arresting police officers at risk of disciplinary action, and/or a civil suit, their resultant conduct will predictably be governed accordingly. If they become aware of a situation where action is warranted, but fear reprisal, the natural tendency is to not act. Such a response is especially likely if they know that ignoring a situation can be done without fear of repercussions. If a pattern of such conduct evolves, relaxed enforcement can result in an increase of offences being committed against the members of the community in question. Accepting that the officer almost certainly does not reside in that neighborhood and therefore will not personally suffer the consequences of an increased crime rate, and accepting that turning a "blind eye" will almost certainly not result in reprisal, one begins to understand why police officers may become apathetic. Internal policies, court rulings, and legislative actions that serve to generate results of the nature described above can be argued to be unfairly discriminatory relative to the class that was intended to be protected.

Unfortunately, results such as those described above have occurred. For example, traffic stops being made by police officers in Minneapolis, Minnesota, dropped by 63 percent when they were accused by the mayor and chief of police of racial profiling. In the year 2000, when the Los Angeles California Police Department came under scrutiny by the Justice Department, relative to racial profiling, arrests declined by 25 percent while homicides increased by a corresponding and alarming 25 percent. In Pittsburgh, Pennsylvania, as a result of a consent decree, police officers are reported to be making arrests based on a racial quota (Mac Donald, 2000).

Illustrating how devastating but predictable adverse responses can be, when scrutiny is perceived to be unreasonable and unfair, not just relative to the profiling issue, consider the following example, a true occurrence featuring informative parallels. There was a situation during the Vietnam war wherein very knowledgeable and skilled Machinist Mates manned the engine room of a Navy war ship. The captain was highly respected by the crew and the ship functioned at the peak of efficiency. Later, that captain was reassigned to a position of greater responsibility and replaced by a new captain, a man bent on finding scapegoats and making examples of people; he caused a notable decrease in the operating efficiency of the ship. Sailors in the engine room, knowing they were at risk of making a mistake through normal human error every time they operated a piece of complex machinery, took the defensive action of denying knowing how to operate many pieces of machinery so as to avoid the risk of making a mistake and being subject to disciplinary action as a result. During the investigation of a mishap that had occurred because of human error, a sailor went to the command and bluntly explained the situation. He explained that sailors had become so paranoid they were denying knowing how to operate critically important pieces of machinery, and that many who had been contemplating reenlistment were then determined to complete their enlistment and return to civilian life. At that point the investigation came to an abrupt halt and no more was heard about it. That sailor, being so candid, put himself at risk of retaliation but the situation had become so acute that he saw it as necessary. The point is, when policies are formulated, when judges make rulings, and when legislators enact laws, it is important to examine not only the problem that is intended to be abated, but also potential and often predictable collateral problems. When the sailors mentioned above went on the defensive, they were not trying to punish anyone. Similarly, when police officers go on the defensive, they are not trying to punish anyone. They are trying to preserve themselves and their career. They are trying to avoid unjust consequences for just actions. Such responses are predictable and should not represent a surprise to any policy maker.

Social pressures can also be detrimental. Not long ago, relative to social unrest (a riot), the Seattle Washington Police Department was accused of acting too quickly, and too harshly. Later, when social unrest again occurred, that police department was accused of not acting quickly enough. A no win situation! What will be their response if another incident of social unrest develops?

Personal political ambitions of many key law enforcement officials, and the politicians to whom they are accountable, is a reality and can create confusion for both officers and the public. Such a political environment often results in the correct response not being the safest or the easiest. That fact is attested to by the case wherein the former Colonel Carl Williams of the New Jersey State Police was terminated by then Governor Christine Todd Whitman for publicly stating that Blacks and Hispanics were most likely to be involved in the trafficking of cocaine and marijuana. His statement, even though supported by current DEA statistics, was not accepted as being politically correct and cost him his job. Such an occurrence puts a chilling effect on other law enforcement officials feeling free to perform their jobs based on facts rather than political pressures. Chief Ortega of the Salt Lake City Utah Police Department suffered a public backlash when he made the statement that illegal immigrants from Mexico were the dominant participants in the trafficking of various illicit drugs in Utah. Such a statement coming from a Hispanic Chief attests to the fact that political correctness is a concern regardless of ones ethnicity or race.

Consent Decrees

If enforcement efforts focus on one class of people while largely ignoring others, arrest rates will incorrectly suggest the target class to be disproportionately involved.

A *consent decree* is a judgement entered into by consent of all parties wherein a defendant agrees to discontinue illegal activity, real or alleged, but without admitting guilt.

Law enforcement has not only seen a dramatic increase in lawsuits filed by citizens, but an increase in lawsuits and/or investigations initiated by the Department of Justice (DOJ). The Department of Justice will often file "pattern and practice" lawsuits under the Equal

Protection Clause of Federal Civil Rights Statutes when they have reason to believe a law enforcement agency is discriminating against certain classes of people. A consent decree will usually require that the departments officers have reasonable suspicion before requesting consent to search (persons, homes, and effects) and that statistics be maintained on all contacts officers make with individuals while executing their duties. Often some other action, to be determined by the DOJ, will also be required.

At the time of this writing, the Columbus Ohio Police Department is in litigation with the Department of Justice, and Eastpointe, Michigan, and Orange County, Florida, is under investigation (Racial Profiling, Issues and Law, 2001). The mere threat of a lawsuit by the Department of Justice will often compel police departments to implement measures to ensure against racial bias. This could include features similar to those found in consent decrees. Two agencies that have entered into consent decrees with the DOJ are the New Jersey State Police and the Maryland State Police.

The New Jersey State Police was allegedly targeting minority motorists suspected of trafficking illicit drugs on the New Jersey State Turnpike. The discrimination was reported to be so pervasive that troopers referred to patrol duty as "riding the black dragon" (Racial Profiling, This Week in Law Enforcement, 2000). A confidential 1989 state police memo reported that minorities were the subject of more stops than whites, and accounted for 60 percent of the arrests on the New Jersey Turnpike. In fact, Blacks and Hispanics drove at least eight out of ten vehicles stopped on the Turnpike during the last decade. The practice at that time wasn't referred to as racial profiling, but was referred to as a "documented criminal phenomenon, rather than racial bias" (Racial Profiling, This Week In Law Enforcement, 2000). Their basis for making that claim were statistics gathered that detailed suspected drug activity by minority groups, mainly Black or Hispanic, labeling them as targets for police. This resulted in increased enforcement and vehicle stops relative to those groups, which in turn resulted in increased arrests. That created the appearance that an increased number of minorities were involved in the drug trade when in fact they may have just been subjected to increased scrutiny resulting in a self-fulfilling prophesy. An analogy would be the city that desires to reduce its crime rate by hiring more officers and, with more officers in the street more arrests are made thus creating the appearance of an increased crime rate. If enforcement efforts focus on one class of people while largely ignoring others, arrest rates will incorrectly suggest the target class to be disproportionately involved. Statistics can be troublesome and, if not accurate, can result in ineffectual and/or errant corrective efforts.

The Maryland State Police agreed to end any "pattern or practice" of race-based drug courier profiling traffic stops, and searches, as part of a settlement in a case brought against them by four black motorists (*Wilkins v. Maryland State Police*, Civ. No. MJG-93-468 USDC MD). Under Maryland's agreement, they are required to begin compiling statistics about the numbers and race of individuals they stop. They additionally will pay $45,600 in legal fees and $12,500 to each of the plaintiffs, and will train their police personnel in the laws of highway interdiction (NewsBriefs, 1995).

Measures similar to those found in consent decrees are often implemented voluntarily by police agencies in an effort to dispel any appearance of racial discrimination. The extent to which they mimic the features of a consent decree will of course vary from one agency to another, and depending upon circumstances. Some may keep statistics on contacts while others may ensure that reasonable suspicion has been met before consent searches are attempted. Often it is smaller agencies that can handle the logistics of compiling statistical information as part of the effort.

Consent decrees can, on the surface, appear to be a justifiable and reasonable means to end patterns and practices of discrimination within an agency. But one must consider the effect it will have on the agency involved, and the community that the officers are entrusted to protect. The logistics of systematically compiling statistical data would no doubt be enormous, requiring increased staff to support the increased workload of "number crunching." One of many concerns is the extent to which officers patrolling beat areas with a higher percentage of minorities will try to "balance their books" by apportioning citations to minority and non-minority citizens in a manner calculated to avoid being labeled a racist. Also, will officers reduce enforcement efforts in minority areas that may be prone to higher levels of criminal activity thereby increasing the potential that citizens residing in the area will become a crime victim? These are just a couple of the legitimate concerns that must be considered before an agency enacts policies that may create more problems than they prevent. The officers of a mid size police department in the Midwest responded to the department's attempt in a predictable way. When officers discovered the reason for the acquisition of data, they quit issuing citations to all classes as a form of protest.

Police departments must enact well-conceived and unambiguous policies relative to discrimination and persecution supported by the selection of high caliber officers and quality supervision. Also essential is frequent and documented training relative to such issues as cultural awareness, racial sensitivity, search and seizure laws, what constitutes reasonable suspicion and probable cause, justifiable use of force, theory of escalation, and proper methods of criminal profiling. In addition, emphasis on public education has merit. Department policy must, of course, require officers to report violations that are witnessed or known to be occurring.

Greater Constitutional Protection

Another trend in American law is that some states are interpreting state constitutional laws differently than the U.S. Constitution. The interpretations are providing greater individual protection to citizens while creating higher standards for law enforcement than what is required by the constitution (Hansen, 2000). The result is officers cannot conduct consent searches of subjects unless reasonable cause has been established which is not in compliance with what the U.S. Constitution provides. Example, New Jersey State Police.

Do Conspiracies to Discriminate Exist?

That racist government was overtly practicing racial discrimination by denying black people the right to be in their community for any reason, and those who ventured into their jurisdiction were subjected to racial persecution in the form of police harassment.

Almost all police officers are honest citizens performing their job to the best of their ability, and they are not governed by racial bias. However, unfortunately, there are exceptions. And, while most police departments, and the governmental body they represent, do not conspire to discriminate, history suggests that it does occur. Case in point. There was a municipality bordering a major northern city, the munic-

ipality in question bordering a neighborhood that was inhabited disproportionately by Black people. The government of that municipality had made it clear that Black people would not flow over the border into their town with that determination enforced by the police
department who historically subjected any Black person found in their
jurisdiction to intense harassment (persecution) by stopping and
detaining them without reasonable suspicion or probable cause. A
Black musician who out of necessity would travel through that community, on the state highway, while commuting to and from work, was
stopped and detained so many times without reasonable suspicion or
probable cause, and without charges being made, that he finally sued
and won.

The Black residents of the neighborhood in question knew very well
to avoid the discriminating municipality; many had confided that real-
ization to one of the authors who, for years, resided in that neighborhood. Also, that situation was sufficiently troublesome that instructors
in the state's police academy, attended by one of the authors, used it
as a bad example, an example of a very racist municipal government.
Again, exclusion was the mechanism, and the government via its
police department ambitiously but illegally enforced it. That racist
government was overtly practicing racial discrimination by denying
Black people the right to be in their community for any reason, and
those who ventured into their jurisdiction were subjected to racial persecution in the form of police harassment. Hence, that is not an example of racial profiling. It is a case of racial discrimination and racial
persecution.

Racial Profiling Data Collection Systems

Many times law enforcement agencies are pressured by politics to
enter into activities that at least on the surface appear to be addressing
a problem. This is apparent when some political figure calls the police
to resolve some problem in their neighborhood whether it is criminal
in nature or a barking dog and want action. Police officers must drop
all their current activities and resolve the problem because of the
important nature of the problem (or is it the important person). Such
is the case with the issue of data collection systems.

This situation is one of the least understood legal actions that are
unduly restrictive for law enforcement. The long-term effects on

crime will eventually reveal the present misapplication of law needed to avoid current litigation (Hansen, 2000).

Political Attempts Relative to Anti-Profiling and Equal Protection

A bill known as the Traffic Stops Statistics Study Act of 1999 was introduced in the United States Senate on April 15, 1999 to provide for the collection of data on traffic stops. The bill was not enacted. A similar bill was introduced in the year 2000 but did not pass. It would have required the attorney general of the United States to conduct a nationwide study of law enforcement traffic stops. In the initial analysis, the attorney general would have performed an initial analysis of existing data, including complaints alleging stops motivated by race or other bias, and other information concerning stops motivated by race and/or other bias. After completion of the initial analysis, the attorney general would gather data on traffic stops from a nationwide sample of jurisdictions, including jurisdictions the attorney general identified in the initial analysis as being involved in alleged discrimination. The data gathered would include the following:

1. The traffic infraction alleged to have been committed that led to the stop.
2. Identifying characteristics of the driver stopped, including the race, gender, ethnicity, and approximate age of the driver.
3. Whether immigration status was questioned, immigration documents were requested, or an inquiry was made to the U.S. Department of Immigration and Naturalization Service with regard to any person in the vehicle.
4. The number of individuals in the stopped vehicle.
5. Whether a search was instituted as a result of the stop and whether consent was requested for the search.
6. Any alleged criminal behavior by the driver that justified the search.
7. Any items seized, including contraband or money.
8. Whether any warning or citation was issued as a result of the stop.
9. Whether an arrest was made as a result of either the stop or the search and the justification for the arrest.
10. The duration of the stop.

The results of the attorney general's initial analysis would have been reported to Congress no later than 120 days after the date of the enactment of the act. The report would have been available to the public, and jurisdictions identified for study would be reported. The study would last for two years, and the results would be reported to Congress.

So why discuss the Traffic Stops Statistics Study Act of 1999 if it was not enacted by Congress? Because of what has resulted from the recognition and misunderstanding of this bill by those in policy making positions. In June of 1999 President Clinton, not wanting to wait for Congress to act, ordered all federal law enforcement agencies to began collecting data on the race and gender of those they arrest. New Jersey Senators Richard Codey and Shirley Turner sponsored and introduced a bill (Senate Concurrent Resolution No. 111) on March 15, 1999, (one month before the Traffic Stops Statistics Study Act of 1999) in the state of New Jersey to end alleged racial profiling. The bill urges the Attorney General of the Unites States to investigate allegations of racial profiling by the New Jersey State Police. The U.S. Attorney General's Office conducting the investigation will lend credibility to the investigation being independent and objective (Senate Concurrent Resolution No. 111, 1999). In addition to New Jersey passing a bill to require data gathering, many other states have passed similar legislation. Some of those states include: Connecticut, Kansas, Missouri and Washington. Hundreds of law enforcement agencies have also voluntarily started to gather data. In California, for example, 75 agencies including the California Highway Patrol (CHP) have begun to implement data collection systems (Ramirez, 2000). As can be seen, the misunderstandings on virtually all levels abound when it comes to a politically and emotionally charged issue such as racial profiling.

Data collection systems have recently been utilized by law enforcement agencies for several reasons. Some agencies have agreed (in lieu of a lawsuit) to gather data as part of a consent decree while others have begun doing it voluntarily for reasons such as maintaining positive community relations.

The data gathered and the systems utilized for data compilation vary depending on the agency. Most agencies that gather data, however, will compile the following statistics:

1. Race or ethnicity
2. Age
3. Gender
4. Reason for the traffic stop

Other data compiled sometimes includes:
1. The disposition of a traffic stop such as whether a citation was issued or an oral or written warning given.
2. Whether an arrest was made.
3. Whether a search was conducted, and the type of search (consent, plain view, inventory, etc.).
4. If drugs or weapons were found.
5. If property was seized.

An increase in the number of factors compiled will, of course, create greater difficulty in analyzing the data.

If the decision is made by an agency to compile data, strong consideration should be given to creating a system that can easily be adapted to current patrol activities. Reducing the time necessary for officers to record data, and keeping it simple, will result in less resistance exhibited by the officers affected. A system currently being utilized by the San Jose California Police Department uses the vehicle's Mobile Data Terminal (MDT) and/or the agency's dispatcher to record/report data. San Jose Police Department gathers only age, gender, race or ethnicity, and the reason for the traffic stop. By gathering such a narrow field of data, their system is adequate, thus resulting in limited cost and officer down time.

Some agencies have implemented systems costing millions of dollars (New Jersey State Police). These systems will often utilize additional equipment such as handheld computers to record data and transmit it to a data bank. However, the more comprehensive the data gathering system is, the greater the resistance to its use. Resistance often results because of the time that is required for recording and transmitting data that the officer deems to be unnecessary. Also, officers are often reluctant to get involved with a program they feel is motivated by political interests and can potentially create more difficulty in an already difficult job. Resistance can sometimes be overcome with training.

Many problems arise with data gathering systems. The systems that tend to work best are those that do not identify the officer or the subject contacted in the data. But even though officers are not identified, many feel they or their districts will be singled out as biased. This brings up another issue. Most agencies that gather data have no quality control. That is to say, they do not conduct crosschecks or random checks of data to see if data is being correctly documented.

Another issue in gathering data is how the race or ethnicity of the subject is determined. Does the officer ask, or assume? Most agencies use the officer's perception of the race or ethnicity of the subject as an indicator. Many agencies feel that if the race or ethnicity of the subject is relevant to a traffic stop, the officer's perception will be the best determinant. But, that is wholly subjective and the question begging an answer is, how does one look at another person and know with any degree of certainty what their ethnicity consists of? And, if the person is asked, problems of multiple ethnicities remain, and asking won't result in factual data when the subject chooses to not disclose their ethnicity.

Difficulties Associated with Data Gathering

In any survey or data gathering effort, those conducting the study must clearly identify their objectives; what is intended to be accomplished? Of the reported hundreds of agencies currently conducting data gathering and spending time and costly resources, there is one grave underlying flaw that remains unresolved. Once the data has been gathered, what is to be done with it? What does the data show? How does it show that there is or is not a racial bias in law enforcement practices? In effect, what does one compare the data against? Of all the agencies that are conducting data gathering, not one has come up with an effective benchmark against which to compare the data. Census polls are often utilized as a benchmark, but are ineffective for determining demographics for profiling reasons. That is because race and/or national origin are not reflected on a driver's license. The ethnicity of drivers cannot be determined from such statistics, and the statistics are also continually changing. Those found on traffic ways passing through an area are also not necessarily a representation of the demographics of the neighborhood itself. Some pro-data gathering advocates make the assertion that an adequate benchmark can be obtained by monitoring the traffic ways. They contend that an analyst could drive the traffic way and observe the percentages of drivers that are driving in excess of a certain determined speed that would likely draw the attention of a police officer. The problems with such a theory are many. Factors that could interfere with such a benchmark are endless, and could include such factors as the time of the day, the day of the week, events that would result in a disproportionate number of one race or ethnicity traveling through the area, and the law enforcement practices of the police officers. Special events can also skew the local ethnic demographics for the duration of the event, which can render invalid any benchmark information that is acquired during that period.

A booklet titled *A Resource Guide on Racial Profiling Data Collection Systems* was prepared by Northwestern University, and was supported by funding from the United States Department of Justice. This document is useful for agencies considering data gathering, and can be obtained from the Department of Justice, or downloaded from the DOJ website. A review of the *Resource Guide* will reveal the many difficulties that are being experienced by agencies currently gathering data. Some of the agencies profiled in the *Resource Guide* include San Jose and San Diego, California, North Carolina, New Jersey, and Great Britain. Many of those agencies are experiencing the same challenges when implementing a data collection system. One of the key challenges is the difficulty in determining an adequate benchmark.

The underlying purpose for gathering and analyzing data is to detect and prevent racial bias on the part of police officers. However, if quality officers are hired, provided quality training, and given the benefit of competent leadership, one is left questioning the extent to which the compilation of statistical data is necessary, or justified from a cost/benefit standpoint.

Human Resource Management
(Selection, Training, and Supervision, of Police Officers)

If quality officers are hired, provided quality training, and given the benefit of competent leadership, one is left questioning the extent to which the compilation of statistical data is necessary, or justified from a cost/benefit standpoint.

This issue has already been addressed, but it is so vitally important that it merits further discussion. Anti-discrimination efforts can be no better than the caliber of the officers that are hired, the quality of the training they are provided, and the quality of management and supervision. And, of course, departmental policies must be well conceived. If those ingredients are not present, efforts to compile statistics will do nothing to solve a problem, even though an uninformed community may be left with the illusion that something worthwhile is being done. And, if monitoring efforts were to disclose a pattern of unfair discrimination, the solution to the problem would be found in reevaluating the criteria for hiring, training, and supervision.

If quality officers are hired, provided quality training, and given the benefit of competent leadership, one is left questioning the extent to which the compilation of statistical data is necessary, or justified from a cost/benefit standpoint. It could be argued that the cost of accumulating and analyzing statistical data is money that would be far more fruitful if applied to quality training. Quality training increases officer competence, which increases confidence, which enhances morale, all of which translates into better community service. Contrast that with police officers that are to varying degrees demoralized by efforts to accumulate statistical data under a chilling cloud of administrative and community distrust.

Anyone who has studied management understands the extent to which employee morale affects the health of an organization, and the extent to which adverse employee morale is a symptom of weak management. Morale affects employee turnover, and significantly affects the quality of job performance not only on the part of individual officers, but also relative to the department as a whole.

Any contemplation of an effort to accumulate statistical data relative to racial bias and discrimination on the part of officers must consider the following:

1. The extent to which the effort will generate reliable results.
2. The potential consequences of subsequently formulating policies on the basis of inaccurate or incomplete information.
3. The monetary cost that will be incurred.
4. The extent to which it will adversely impose upon officers who are already very busy.
5. The impact it will have on officer morale.

6. How officers will in fact rather than theory respond to the effort.
7. How it will in the final analysis affect the quality of community service.

Having considered the above concerns, one should revisit the issue of quality selection, training, and supervision, coupled with a properly staffed and trained Internal Affairs Department to investigate situations on a case by case basis as they present themselves.

When an officer has been given the benefit of quality training and competent leadership, and they commit an act of discrimination, blame can be assigned to that officer. But, if that officer has not been provided quality training, and leadership is weak, blame must also be assigned to the administration irrespective of any data acquisition efforts that may be in effect. Compiling statistical data may have merit when the program has been properly conceived and implemented, but such an effort has little merit if poorly conceived and executed, and done in the absence of quality selection, training, and leadership.

When law enforcement administrators prepare budget proposals they are competing for limited funds. Police departments must operate within their budget and therefore it is important to consider the extent to which the cost of acquiring and analyzing statistical data will dilute funds that would otherwise be available for quality training. As always, when seeking a solution for an existing problem, and when considering preventive measures for potential problems, it is better to act than react.

Ethics and Law Enforcement

If an officer's integrity or judgment is impeached, the officer may become useless in court, and thus on the street.

If hiring criteria does not result in high caliber officers, quality training is not provided, and supervision is weak, mistakes on the part of police officers are more likely, as are problems of ethics. Training must include emphasis on the need to maintain integrity and bias free enforcement. Defense attorneys are capturing the personnel files of police officers, via subpoena, in an attempt to impeach their credibility. Defense attorneys are looking for evidence of discipline or complaints against the officer relative to racial bias, lack of integrity, conduct unbecoming, and criminal conduct. Officers that have received discipline for racial discrimination will no doubt be impeached with that evidence when testifying as a witness against a minority defendant (Hansen, 2000). An officer is required as a part of their duties, and often under subpoena, to testify in court. When an officer's integrity and/or judgment is impeached, the officer may become useless in court, and thus on the street. Therefore police executives should become less tolerant and less willing to retain an officer who is disciplined for being untruthful or demonstrating bias (Hansen, 2000).

Selective Prosecution of Minorities (Case Study)

Selective enforcement and prosecution occurs, but more often it is simply alleged. Earlier, relative to pretext stops, there was brief discussion relative to such stops as they pertain to Fourth and Fourteenth Amendment rights. In this section, excerpts are presented that have been taken directly from the court case ruling, *U.S. v. Armstrong*, decided May 13th, 1996.

Case Summary

In response to their indictment on "crack" cocaine and other federal charges, respondents filed a motion for discovery or for dismissal, alleging that they were selected for prosecution because they are Black. The District Court granted the motion over the Government's argument, among others, that there was no evidence or allegation that it had failed to prosecute non-Black defendants. When the Government indicated it would not comply with the discovery order, the court dismissed the case. The en banc Ninth Circuit affirmed, holding that the proof requirements for a selective prosecution claim do not compel a defendant to demonstrate that the Government has failed to prosecute others who are similarly situated (End of Summary).

The court held for a defendant to be entitled to discovery on a claim that he was singled out for prosecution on the basis of his race, he must make a threshold showing that the Government declined to prosecute similarly situated suspects of other races.

Chief Justice Rehnquist delivered the opinion of the court: In this case, we consider the showing necessary for a defendant to be entitled to discovery on a claim that the prosecuting attorney singled him out for prosecution on the basis of his race. We conclude that respondents failed to satisfy the threshold show-ing: They failed to show that the Government declined to prosecute similarly situated suspects of other races.

In April 1992, respondents were indicted in the United States District Court for the Central District of California on charges of conspiring to possess with intent to distribute more than 50 grams of cocaine base (crack) and conspiring to distribute the same, in violation of 21 U.S. Ct. 841 and 846 (1988 ed. and Supp. IV), and federal firearms offenses. For three months prior to the indict-ment, agents of the Federal Bureau of Alcohol, Tobacco, and Firearms and the Narcotics Division of the Inglewood California Police Department had infil-trated a suspected crack distribution ring by using three confidential inform-ants. On seven separate occasions during this period, the informants had bought a total of 124.3 grams of crack from respondents and witnessed respondents car-rying firearms during the sales. The agents searched the hotel room in which the sales were transacted, arrested respondents Armstrong and Hampton in the room, and found more crack and a loaded gun. The agents later arrested the other respondents as part of the ring.

In response to the indictment, respondents filed a motion for discovery or for dismissal of the indictment, alleging that they were selected for federal prosecu-tion because they are Black. In support of their motion, they offered only an affidavit by a paralegal specialist, employed by the Office of the Federal Public Defender representing one of the respondents. The only allegation in the affi-davit was that, in every one of the 24 841 or 846 cases closed by the office dur-ing 1991, the defendant was Black. Accompanying the affidavit was a study listing the 24 defendants, their race, whether they were prosecuted for dealing cocaine as well as crack, and the status of each case.

The Government opposed the discovery motion, arguing, among other things, that there was no evidence or allegation that the Government has acted unfair-ly or has prosecuted non-Black defendants or failed to prosecute them. The District Court granted the motion. It ordered the Government (1) to provide a list of all cases from the last three years in which the Government charged both cocaine and firearms offenses, (2) to identify the race of the defendants in those cases, (3) to identify what levels of law enforcement were involved in the inves-tigations of those cases, and (4) to explain its criteria for deciding to prosecute those defendants for federal cocaine offenses.

The Government moved for reconsideration of the District Court's discovery order. With this motion it submitted affidavits and other evidence to explain why it had chosen to prosecute respondents and why respondents' study did not support the inference that the Government was singling out Blacks for cocaine prosecution. The federal and local agents participating in the case alleged in affidavits that race played no role in their investigation. An Assistant United States Attorney explained in an affidavit that the decision to prosecute met the general criteria for prosecution, because there was over 100 grams of cocaine base involved, over twice the threshold necessary for a ten year mandatory minimum sentence; there were multiple sales involving multiple defendants, thereby indicating a fairly substantial crack cocaine ring; . . . there were multiple federal firearms violations intertwined with the narcotics trafficking; the overall evidence in the case was extremely strong, including audio and videotapes of defendants; . . . and several of the defendants had criminal histories including narcotics and firearms violations.

The Government also submitted sections of a published 1989 Drug Enforcement Administration report which concluded that large-scale, interstate trafficking networks controlled by Jamaicans, Haitians and Black street gangs dominate the manufacture and distribution of crack. (J. Featherly & E. Hill, Crack Cocaine Overview 1989; App. 103).

The Court of Appeals reached its decision in part because it started with the presumption that people of all races commit all types of crimes not with the premise that any type of crime is the exclusive province of any particular racial or ethnic group. 48 F.3d, at 1516-1517. It cited no authority for this proposition, which seems contradicted by the most recent statistics of the United States Sentencing Commission. Those statistics show that: More than 90 percent of the persons sentenced in 1994 for crack cocaine trafficking were Black, United States Sentencing Comm'n, 1994 Annual Report 107 (Table 45); 93.4 percent of convicted LSD dealers were White, ibid.; and 91 percent of those convicted for pornography or prostitution were White, id., at 41 (Table 13). Presumptions at war with presumably reliable statistics have no proper place in the analysis of this issue.

The Court of Appeals also expressed concern about the "evidentiary obstacles defendants face." [Citations omitted]. But all of its sister circuits that have confronted the issue have required that defendants produce some evidence of differential treatment of similarly situated members of other races or protected classes. In the present case, if the claim of selective prosecution were well founded, it should not have been an insuperable task to prove that persons of other races were being treated differently than respondents. For instance, respondents could have investigated whether similarly situated persons of other races were prosecuted by the state of California, were known to federal law enforcement officers, but were not prosecuted in federal court. We think the required threshold— a credible showing of different treatment of similarly situated persons—ade-

quately balances the Government's interest in vigorous prosecution and the defendant's interest in avoiding selective prosecution.

In *U.S. v. Armstrong*, a Federal Court case involving a defendant arrested for possession of crack cocaine, the court provided some insight into how the courts may consider law enforcement's use of race or ethnicity as a basis for enforcement action. Is there racial disparity in the commission of different types of crime? Sure there is, but often police executives are hesitant to utilize the obvious racial distinctions in criminal behavior for devising effective law enforcement strategies because of the political backlash that will certainly result if the tactics are discovered. Consider the courts view on race or ethnicity as a basis for enforcement and you will discover that the courts are often insulated from politically correct pressure, whereas police officials are not. Could it be that Supreme Court Justices are appointed for life, while police executives are not, thus resulting in police executives being more concerned about politically sensitive issues?

Challenge to Drug Profile Stops
(Alleged 14th Amendment Rights Violation)

In *U.S. v. Avery* the Sixth Circuit Court of Appeals ruled that a defendant was required to prove that he or she was contacted by law enforcement based solely because of his or her race.

On December 16, 1993, agents of the Cincinnati/Northern Kentucky Airport Narcotics Interdiction Unit were monitoring a flight from Los Angeles. Because their observations did not provoke concern, they proceeded toward a different concourse. As they walked through a tunnel in the direction of the concourse, one of the officers noticed Cortez Avery walking hurriedly and stated to his fellow officers, "wait a minute, guys, let this guy get by us." (Citations omitted). Avery, a young African-American male, was wearing sweat pants and a short-sleeve sweatshirt and was carrying a duffel carry-on bag. According to the officer, Avery appeared very focused and looked straight ahead. The officer stated, "[Avery] looked like a man on a mission." The officers decided to follow Avery.

Avery stopped at a gate, went to an empty row of seats facing the windows, and sat in the seat that was closest to the departure door. He presented his boarding pass to the agent at the counter before a boarding announcement was made and was the first passenger to board the plane. Avery's actions appeared peculiar to the officer up to that point, so he retrieved Avery's boarding pass after Avery boarded and asked the gate agent for ticketing information. The agent indicated that Avery used a one-way ticket purchased with cash thirty-five minutes prior to departure from San Juan, Puerto Rico, connecting in Orlando and Cincinnati with the final destination of Washington, D.C. The ticket was not issued in Avery's name, but was in the name of Antoine Jones.

With this information, the officer believed he had "reasonable suspicion" and decided to speak with Avery. Two officers boarded the plane and located Avery in a window seat near the rear of the aircraft. From the aisle behind Avery, the officer identified himself as a police officer, displayed his badge, and asked Avery if he could speak to him. Avery agreed, and the two stepped into the galley at the officer's request. The officers did not block Avery's passageway, however, passengers may have impeded Avery's exit from the plane.

The officer asked Avery if he could see his ticket, but Avery stated that he had thrown it away. He asked Avery where he had come from, and Avery responded that he was traveling from Orlando. The officer then asked Avery if he had been anywhere prior to Orlando, and Avery stated that he had not. In response to the officer's questions concerning the purpose of his visit to Orlando, Avery replied that he had gone to visit friends and was on a mini vacation by himself. Avery said that he lodged at a hotel but could not remember its name; Avery did not have any receipts for the hotel. He also stated that he did not rent a car while in Orlando. The officer then asked the defendant his name, and he identified himself as Cortez Avery. In response to a request for identification, Avery explained that he had none, but gave his correct date of birth, social security number, and address. With regard to the disparity in names, Avery responded that the airline must have made a mistake when it issued the ticket in the name of Antoine Jones.

Avery consented to a search of his person, but refused consent to search the duffel bag. The officer told Avery that he was free to leave, but that the bag would be seized for reasonable suspicion, and a search warrant would be obtained. Avery continued his flight to Washington, D.C., National Airport. The bag was taken to a room and placed amongst other bags. A drug dog was used and the dog indicated a positive alert for drugs giving the officers probable cause. A search warrant was obtained and the bag revealed approximately two kilograms of cocaine. Avery was arrested when he arrived at Washington National Airport.

Avery contended that he was approached and detained solely on the basis of his race. Although he provided statistical evidence (provided by the government concerning 1993–1994 Investigative Contacts and Dispatched Runs) of the disproportionate numbers of Blacks stopped at the airport, his data failed to include the percentage of Blacks traveling by air through the airport. This is a common theme with police departments utilizing data gathering systems to dispel anecdotal evidence of racial bias; there is no benchmark against which to compare gathered data. Avery also failed to provide evidence that black passengers were singled out for investigation in o/v (on-view) cases at a disproportionate rate. The Court replied:

"Avery asks the court to focus specifically and only on the percentage of the total "on-view" contacts that involve blacks compared to the estimated percentage of blacks among the air traveling public. We agree that these numbers are the heart of his statistical argument. The "on-view" cases involve situations in which an officer simply watches passengers in the terminal or passengers deplaning a given flight, and, based on his observations, the officer begins to investigate. "On-view" cases also involve situations wherein the officer obtains a passenger list and looks for passengers connecting from a given flight to certain outbound flights. Although it has been asserted that statistics of the second type of "on-view" cases are not relevant because officers would have no control over the race of a person in the second type of "on-view" case, we do not agree with that supposition. As noted earlier, if officers focused only on Hispanic or other ethnic surnames in choosing the individuals to investigate, not only would they be able to control the investigated population, they could do it with impermissible criteria.

"Approximately 52 percent of all reported cases were 'on-view,' and slightly more than 53 percent of all 'on-view' cases involved blacks. The defendant did not provide a figure for the total percentage of blacks among the air-traveling public. He merely stated that blacks were 'a minority' of the air traveling public. Further, we have no information describing how individuals investigated were chosen in the 'on-view' cases in which the passenger list was used. If we eliminate those 'passenger-list' cases, estimated to account for 50 percent of all 'on-view' cases, we are left with only one-fourth of the cases reported. Moreover, Lt. Blackburn's testimony indicated that a large percentage of unreported contacts were those at the pre-contact investigation stage. Thus, the remaining statistics are circumscribed and 'skewed in that most of the reports involve individuals actually encountered by the officers and not merely investigated at the pre-contact stage.' [Citation omitted] (Magistrate Judge's Report and Recommendation). These statistics simply are not persuasive.

"Investigations targeting a certain race or ethnicity is morally and ethically wrong if the reason for the investigation is solely because of the persons race. This type of enforcement practice is prohibited. When race is a relevant factor to a criminal profile, the courts do not denounce the use of race as long as it does not result in an unfair application of the laws." (*U.S. v. Avery*). The court further stated, "surveillance cannot be challenged under the Fourth Amendment, however, prohibits agents from engaging in investigative surveillance of an individual based solely on impermissible factors such as race." (*U.S. v. Avery*)

Section II

CULTURAL AWARENESS

Chapter 4

UNDERSTANDING SOCIAL CLASSES
AND CULTURES

Without an understanding of various social classes and cultures it is impossible to examine the issues of profiling and discrimination to any meaningful extent.

Introduction

The information provided here in Chapter 4, and also in Chapter 5, will be found in introductory level college courses in psychology and sociology. However, the information is included here, as support material, because it is so germane to the issue of profiling. However, that which is provided is very subject specific, and very much in synopsis form. When considering the issue of profiling and discrimination, one is dealing with people and people related problems and the better informed one is relative to the disciplines of psychology and sociology the better equipped one will be to exercise quality judgment when profiling. Accordingly, college level courses in psychology and sociology are highly recommended.

Without an understanding of various social classes and cultures it is impossible to examine the issues of profiling and discrimination to any meaningful extent. Such an understanding is essential because it is people and their varied status that gives rise to such practices. If there were only one culture in existence, would there be no discrimination and persecution, no conflict? Discrimination would probably still occur relative to such things as age, sex, disability, and socioeconomic status. But, in actuality, there is not a single culture. In almost all countries, especially in the United States, there are numerous cultures and subcultures. In the United States there are an estimated 88 different cultures and languages (Law Enforcement Television, 1993). Because there is such diversity, there will always be those who feel antagonistic towards those perceived to be different. Thus, discrimination and persecution will always occur. And, accepting that there are an estimated 88 different cultures in the United States, the apparent cultural diversity becomes even greater when adding subcultures and class stratification to the equation.

While officially the U.S. has no "caste" system, there is very much an informal caste system although it is not a rigid system into which one is born and above which one cannot rise, as is characteristic of castes found in India. Evidence of an informal but very real social caste system in the U.S. will be found in such labels as "trailer trash," "scooter trash," "white trash," "low class," "working class," "middle class," and "upper class."

There is nothing intrinsically wrong with social stratification, and it has occurred throughout world history and continues. But, problems associated with class stratification do result. Under communism there was, in theory, one class of people; everyone was equal. In reality it was very different and there was very much the ideal culture and the real culture, a concept to be discussed later. An attempt to eliminate the concept of varied social classes would, to some degree, be an attempt to eliminate human nature. Under communism the element of individual incentive was seriously diminished and, in the end, as history has proven, communism did not work as intended. Quasi-religious cults succeed in eliminating human nature through a process of programming and dehumanization wherein the member's resolution is suppressed and they become to varying degrees morally and emotionally anesthetized, and they lose the ability to empathize. Wherever and whenever the human nature element has been eliminated there has been a high and detrimental cost associated with the result. In the end, only partial success has been realized with attempts to minimize differences relative to social stratification.

The college educated professional person certainly feels superior to the landscape maintenance person he or she has hired and, similarly, the landscape maintenance person views the professional person as their social superior. The surgeon feels superior to the operating room staff, and the operating room staff accepts the surgeon's superiority. In both examples, social interaction on anything but a superficial level does not tend to occur. A surgeon, a successful attorney, and the CEO of a large and successful company would be likely to view one another as peers. But, even within classes there is social stratum. For example, an attorney once explained that attorneys are not equal within their class and a very definite "pecking order" exists. Some attorneys are skilled and economically successful while others are not. The same phenomena hold true for medical doctors, and some enjoy a higher status by virtue of their specialty within the medical field. A chiropractor, no matter how successful, will never enjoy the same professional and social status, as does a successful surgeon.

Almost everyone has heard the phrase "keeping up with the Jones'." The phrase refers to people labeled as social climbers. Social combers are characterized as people trying to appear to be equal to someone whose economic success and resultant social status exceeds their own. One must wonder how many new vehicles are purchased because someone the buyer knows has purchased a new vehicle and they desire to remain equal. In such cases the underlying motive to purchase a new vehicle is to either enhance their apparent social status, or to avoid a declining social status. New and expensive vehicles are a symbol of success for many people. Conversely, an older vehicle symbolizes marginal success. For many, an older vehicle is unacceptable for social reasons. People are acutely aware of social status and who belongs where in the hierarchy. And a great deal of effort and money is often spent in response to that awareness.

It was stated earlier that the social caste system in the U.S. is not as rigid as the hereditary Hindu social castes found in India, but it is rigid nonetheless. In the U.S., if a medical doctor were to marry a working class person, the working class spouse is not, by virtue of the marriage, elevated to the social status of the doctor. But, neither is the doctor reduced to the working class status. But, such a union can to varying degrees result in a loss of professional and/or social prestige enjoyed by the doctor, and a somewhat elevated level of prestige enjoyed by the working class spouse. The doctor is likely to find that attending social functions with their working class spouse will in many instances be accompanied by social discomfort, and in some cases the spouse may not be included. A young lady with a college degree and successful white-collar (professional) career will almost certainly encounter opposition from family and friends if she expresses an intent to marry the non-degreed young man working at the grocery store stocking shelves and bagging groceries.

Evidence of a social caste system in the U.S. will also be found in the tendency of many who grew up in one class but through education and hard work coupled with luck achieved a higher social class status, to categorically reject former friends who remain in the lower class, or to treat those friends in a conspicuously condescending manner. Commonly, the person having succeeded in elevating him or herself socially will go to extraordinary lengths to publicly reflect that success or, in other words, flaunt it. It is also common for the spouse, who may have had little or nothing to do with the success that has been achieved, to embrace the higher status without regard for the fact that without the successful spouse they would not be where they are. In fact, they would plunge to their lower social status without the successful spouse.

In the final analysis, although the U.S. is not generally considered to have a social caste system characteristic of the Hindu social caste system found in India, at least not officially, there very much is a caste system in place although it is generally referred to as social class. It is also referred to as social stratification and class stratification.

Socioeconomic Classes

In the United States, there are different socioeconomic classes of people. While there are different ways to categorize them, for purposes of this analysis it will be considered that there is the (1) under class, (2) low class, (3) working class, (4) lower middle class, (5) upper middle class, and (6) the upper class. This discussion is brief but is offered for familiarization purposes. College level courses in sociology are highly recommended.

The underclass is characterized by, but not limited to, inner-city residents caught up in a cycle of complete poverty that has persisted for a generation or more. They are by any measure the poorest of the poor with almost no hope to rise above their station. This group features unskilled people who are underemployed, unemployed, and many who have never been employed. In this group one will find single mothers on welfare, children growing up in welfare dependent homes, and the homeless. The people are universally poorly educated and occupy crime ridden impoverished neighborhoods.

The low class is characterized by low income people, many unemployed, many working unskilled manufacturing or service jobs, full or part time with most being part time. Most live in cities with very few owning their own home. Those who have an automobile will have acquired it used. The low class is disproportionately non-White. Homeless people will also be found in this category.

The working class is characterized by male and female laborers who work for modest wages with two income families being common out of necessity. This class is racially and ethnically diverse with college education being the exception. Older members may own their own home but it is usually in a low income neighborhood, but most of the younger ones rent. Their vehicles are commonly fairly late model but a lower priced model. The people of this class are commonly employed in positions labeled blue collar. They work as factory workers, office workers, mechanics, sales clerks, and restaurant workers. Their children tend not to pursue education beyond high school but, rather, seek employment once out of high school. Many drop out of high school.

The lower middle class is characterized by people in the lower portion of the average income range. Most have a high school education and some have completed college. Many rent and those who own homes tend to own a moderately priced home. They tend to drive late model vehicles in the moderate price range. People in this category will be found working as nurses, sales people, schoolteachers, police officers, and skilled jobs in offices. Most encourage their children to attend college.

The upper middle class is characterized by high income professional and managerial people. Many have completed college on the baccalaureate and graduate level, and many own their own business. Their income is in the upper portion of the average income range. They tend to own nice homes in affluent areas. Almost none rent. They drive new or late model vehicles, often luxury models. Most of their children complete college. In addition to the income derived from their occupation, they tend to have a variety of investments.

The upper class is characterized by extreme wealth. In this class will be found the heads of major corporations, and people who have realized substantial success through investments. Some inherited their money. For most, a substantial portion of their income is derived from investments, stocks, bonds, and real estate. The upper class tends to be politically influential with many of them knowing politicians. They tend to donate campaign money, and they also tend to donate substantial sums to a variety of charities. Some people are born into the upper class while others, with some luck and hard work, negotiate their way into this class.

Ambiguity in Social Class Assignment

When considering classes, things are not always what they appear to be inasmuch as it is easy to assign someone to the wrong class. In other words, one may appear to most appropriately belong to one class while in fact belonging to another, and overlap occurs. Also, there is the tendency for many people to devote considerable effort, and to go deeply into debt, trying to appear to be higher class than they in fact are.

In the upper class there are those who were born into it, and there are those who through hard work and planning coupled with luck achieved wealth sufficient to end up in that category. But, there is a difference between how those who were born into the upper class view themselves, versus how they view those who are new comers. The latter has an income that enables them, entitles them, to move within certain social circles, but they will never completely share the same values. They will always retain, to varying degrees, the values of the class from whence they came. As one sociologist once said, "what you are is where you were when value programmed." In the final analysis, it may be said that there are those who are truly upper class, and there are those who are middle class with an upper class income. The latter will never completely think and feel as the former inasmuch as they don't share the same underlying values, although with time many values will diminish as new values are absorbed.

Value-Stretch

Little needs to be said, but one should understand what sociologists refer to as value-stretch. That phenomenon will be found with many cultures and subcultures that live within yet to varying degrees exist on the fringes of settled (mainstream) society. While the members of such groups do not share all of the values of the dominant society, they embrace most of the general values. However, they also embrace the values unique to their own group that represent, to varying degrees, a departure from the mainstream value system. The result is a value system that is broader in scope than that of the mainstream. Hence, the term value stretch.

Multiple Ethnicities

Multiple ethnicities are a factor that is often overlooked when contemplating the issue of profiling and discrimination. Too often there is a tendency to think of people as being Black, Hispanic, White, Asian, etc. However, many people represent more than just one ethnicity. Most people in the U.S. are a combination of two or more nationalities. If one or more elements of their heritage are that of a protected class, they are entitled to protection for each under the law. For simplicity of discussion, it will be assumed that people feature only one or two national origins.

While a person featuring dual ethnicity may function within both cultures, they will generally lean more towards one than the other for a variety of reasons, most notable being the one in which they were socialized. But, there are some who divide their time between the two and therefore absorb the cultural values of both, often speaking both languages.

Sometimes, they are raised in one culture, having little or no contact with the other, but their genetics will leave them thinking and feeling more like the other. For example, a person who is half Black and half American Indian may be raised in the Black community but, as the individual grows and matures into adulthood, they may find that they think and feel more like an Indian. This can occur irrespective of which nationality they look more like.

The extent to which genetics influences nationality characteristics undoubtedly varies. Studies have been done with twins raised apart to determine the extent to which they are alike even though having been raised in different environments. While there is much that is different by virtue of having been raised in different environments, they tend to demonstrate similarities sufficient to suggest that genetics are also a factor. Why, when the Gypsies have assimilated as many "outsiders" as they have, and have occupied so many different countries over the generations, have they retained so many identifiable and conspicuous characteristics irrespective of the country in which they are found? In each country they are different, as expected, yet in many respects they are also similar. Is there a dominant gene that the mixing of blood tends to not diminish?

Passing

That there are many people who possess multiple ethnicities is a fact. Also a fact is the tendency to reflect some ethnic characteristics stronger than others. It is also true that people tend to identify with one aspect of their heritage more than others. But, it is also true that irrespective of which heritage a person most closely identifies, a person will often present themselves as either one or the other depending upon circumstances. Sometimes when their appearance permits, they will even present themselves as a nationality other than their own. This behavior is referred to as *passing,* passing as one aspect of their heritage, or another, or passing as a member of an ethnic group of which they are not a part.

A person who is half American Indian and half Mexican may choose to pass as an Indian under one set of circumstances, and later pass as a Mexican under a different set of circumstances. Commonly Gypsies pass as some other nationality to avoid the discrimination and persecution to which Gypsies are subjected. For example, one family passes as White, but if asked by outsiders to be more specific they will claim to be a mixture of English, Irish, and French. Significantly, relative to that which is referred to as passing, and relative to geography, one does not venture very far into that families lineage, as reflected in their family records, and Spanish names begin appearing.

Culture vs. Subculture

There is a difference between a culture and a subculture. Culture can be defined by the characteristic norms, values, practices, and ethnicity of a group. Subcultures also reflect norms, values, and practices characteristic of the group. However, subculture boundaries are not distinguished along ethnic lines. For example, Italians represent a culture, as do Lapps, Chinese, Mexicans, Jews, and Gypsies. Bikers are an example of a subculture. A subculture can be said to be a culture that exists within or, more appropriately stated, on the fringes of the dominant culture yet differs from the mainstream in one or more important ways.

Just as cultures feature variations within the larger culture, the same is true for subcultures. Spanish and German Gypsies are both European Gypsies and share a common ethnic heritage. However, each has assimilated different norms and values in their travel to their current homes. European Gypsies differ notably from American Gypsies for the same reason. And, American Gypsies differ depending upon the tribe from which they have emanated, and the extent to which they have maintained cultural/tribal affiliations. One would also find notable differences between Russian and American Jews. The biker subculture features notable strata of subcultures within the subculture.

Ideal Culture vs. Real Culture

Any given culture will have a dominant system of values and norms, but that culture will also feature many contradictions. Hence, a culture will feature that which is referred to as ideal culture and real culture. For example, in the United States, the government and most members of mainstream society claim to believe in pluralism. That is, the belief that the members of various cultures should be free to live according to the norms of their culture. That professed set of values represents the ideal culture. In practice, however, the opposite occurs to a notable extent and represents the real culture. In spite of professed values (ideal culture), the real culture manifests itself through ethnocentrism with a notable intolerance for cultures (and subcultures) that feature customs and practices that differ from that of the majority. Hence, in America there is the ideal of equality and pluralism that is contradicted by the reality of instances of discrimination and persecution.

Cultures also feature contradictions in other ways. For example, in the United States, value is placed on individual achievement, but emphasis is also placed upon family values and group unity. To varying degrees the one value conflicts with the other. The former is rooted in individualism while the latter is rooted in a micro sense of community. Hence, the individual who leans more towards one is in conflict with the other.

Culture-lag

Culture-lag occurs when different aspects of a culture change at different rates relative to external circumstances such as technology, economics, and social attitudes. These changes affect individuals within a culture by requiring adjustment of norms and values. Culture-lag permeates American society, and is very apparent in many religions. As society changes with the times, so does religion. Changing with the times is occurring among many previously socially isolated religious orders and is even occurring with the Amish who have been the most isolated of all. The dogmatic value systems associated with most religions coupled with changing socioeconomic conditions present a unique opportunity to study cultural-lag and the differences between ideal and real culture.

Culture-lag can create discomfort and anxiety for members of a culture who disapprove of the changes that are occurring within their culture. This is true for members of the dominant mainstream society, for members of religious orders, and for minorities. However, culture-lag can create deeper levels of frustration for members of minority groups living within the larger and dominant mainstream society. Discomfort results when they are caught between the values and economic forces of the dominant society and the lingering traditional values and norms of their own culture.

Most people have heard older people complain that the younger generation has lost sight of the values they themselves grew up with. When the values of the younger generation depart from those of the elders, conflict results, and we see culture-lag occurring. Young Hispanic people can experience difficulties when they attend mainstream schools, begin adding non-Hispanic people to their inventory of friends, and take jobs within the dominant society. They find that some of the mainstream values and practices are to their liking, and are in some cases necessary. But, when the assimilation includes values that are contrary to their traditional values, conflict results. Young Hispanic people departing from traditional values, to whatever degree, at whatever rate, are contributing to culture-lag. Discomfort is predictable considering they no longer completely internalize the norms of their culture, and neither do they completely internalize the norms of the dominant society. Culture conflict is a predictable result.

As troubling as change is to many people, change is inevitable and all cultures change with time. Each person within a culture changes at different rates and to different degrees. The first immigrants to a new country bring with them their values, and those values will be passed on to their children. But, with each generation fewer of the old values are retained and practiced as they are replaced with, or supplemented with, values that are to varying degrees characteristic of the dominant society of the new country. Hence, how a minority member feels about various social issues will vary depending upon where they fit into the process of cross-cultural values and culture-lag.

One sociologist asserted that when Gypsies, who historically were to varying degrees migratory, became sedentary they suffered erosion of their culture and, in the end, became detribalized and evolved into a hybrid subculture. While in many respects that can be argued to be true, it must be examined within the larger perspective of cross-cultural programming and culture-lag. Gypsies in various countries have much in common one with another but each is also very different by virtue of living in different countries and coexisting with a different dominant culture. And, Gypsies in each country experience culture-lag just as the dominant culture on whose fringes they live experience culture-lag.

Culture-lag occurs with all cultures and, as a result, any culture as it exists today is different than it was 100 years ago, or even 50 years ago. Italians in Italy are not entirely the same today as they were 50 years ago, and neither are we in America the same today as our grand parents were when they were our age. Each lived under a different set of circumstances socially, economically, legally, technologically, etc. But, when a historically migratory people become sedentary there tends to be an increased incidence of their young people marrying outside their culture and that certainly does result in varying degrees of cultural erosion. In the final analysis, it can be said that marrying outside a culture will result in varying degrees of cultural erosion, but just the fact that an historically migratory people becomes sedentary does not in and of itself result in cultural erosion, and neither does adapting to external forces.

With the Gypsy, becoming sedentary does not in any significant way alter the Gypsy-gauje relationship socially, and while the Gypsies lifestyle certainly is to varying degrees different when sedentary as compared with what it was while migratory, that does not justify the assertion that they have suffered detribalization and cultural erosion sufficient to reduce them from a culture to a hybrid subculture. Their cultural values and traditions remain with the persistent social and ideological barriers separating them from the gauje (non-gypsy) diminishing the extent to which the norms and values of the dominant society will erode their culture, although admittedly in some cases it does, such as when the young marry outside the culture.

It would be unfair and inaccurate to say that Italian-Americans, because they live a life that is different from that of their relatives in the old country (Italy), and because their life is different from what it was when their grandparents first settled in the U.S., have become a hybrid subculture and are, therefore, no longer a culture. The same can be said for the Irish-Americans, Asian Americans, etc. So it is with the Gypsy; their becoming sedentary does not reduce them to the status of hybrid subculture. Additionally, accepting that a culture features both visible and hidden elements, logic would suggest that while the visible elements may change as the members of a culture adapt to external circumstances, such a change occurring is not a valid basis upon which to assume that the hidden elements of the culture have to any significant degree also changed. At any rate, the outside observer is poorly equipped to evaluate to what extent the internal order may have changed in response to the forces causing a change in the visible aspects.

The reader should contemplate the rationale underlying what has been said because it is an issue that can be argued many ways. But, perhaps, to debate the issue effectively one must first define what constitutes culture-lag versus cultural erosion, and the extent to which a culture adapting to ever changing external forces such as technology, the economy, laws, and social forces, is demonstrating adaptation and evolution as opposed to erosive deterioration.

Chapter 5

DEVIANCY, OUTSIDERS,
AND DISCRIMINATION

Deviant behavior can be defined as any behavior that is inconsistent with the norms and values of the culture within which it occurs irrespective of whether the behavior is legal or illegal.

Introduction

Having examined social classes and cultures in the previous chapter, a brief examination will be made of some prominent factors frequently underlying racist discrimination and persecution, concepts with which the reader should be familiar considering that when the issue of racial profiling is entertained, it is usually with the assumption that it is an unfairly discriminatory practice. An examination will also be made relative to who discriminates, whether discrimination is always wrong, what constitutes deviant behavior, and what justifies the assertion that society creates outsiders.

Because the focus of this book is discrimination and persecution as it pertains to profiling, one should consider how minorities versus non-minorities perceive the issue. The following is from a year 2000 Gallup poll.

1. **Q:** Is racial profiling widespread?
   A: Yes.   White: 56%.   Black: 77%.
2. **Q:** Have you ever been stopped by police because of race or ethnicity?
   A: Yes.   White: 6%.   Black: 42%.

91

Terms and Concepts Pertinent To the Issue of
Discrimination & Persecution

Acculturation occurs when one adopts the norms and values of the dominant culture, when a person or group is assimilated into the mainstream. See assimilation.

Antisocial Personality Disorder, previously called psychopathic personality disorder, will often be found in those who practice racist discrimination, which is not surprising when examining the following list of classical symptoms. Contemplation of the symptoms leaves it clear that more than anything else it is the ability, or inability, to feel guilt that separates the psychopath from those who are not.

1. Often appears vivacious when first meeting them, charismatic.
2. Lack of social conscience.
3. Incapable of feeling guilt.
4. Cheats and steals.
5. Chronic liars but very convincing when lying.
6. Selfish/self-centered.
7. Lack of impulse control.
8. Emotionally shallow.
9. Manipulates other people.
10. History of impaired interpersonal relationships.

Assimilation is the process by which various cultures are absorbed into the culture of the dominant (mainstream) society. See acculturation.

Bias is a leaning or inclination in some particular direction, often with a disregard for accuracy, or for information suggesting incorrectness. Everyone is biased about certain things. Although bias is not intrinsically wrong, bias is wrong when it hurts someone or it interferes with a person's freedom. A couple that is completely in love and oblivious to the faults of each other while focusing on that which they love, is biased. The result of this bias is a harmonious union. The mother who believes her baby to be the most beautiful child in the world is biased. These examples show that not only is bias acceptable, but sometimes even has positive results. Often, however, bias is detrimental as it leaves one with an inaccurate view of some issue. Biased people, especially relative to issues such as ethnocentrism, tend to have overly simplistic views and are typically resistant to any evidence that contradicts their views.

Bigot. A bigot can be defined as a narrow-minded and prejudiced person who is blindly and intolerantly committed to a rigid opinion relative to issues such as politics, religion and race.

Culture-lag occurs when different aspects of a culture change at different rates relative to external circumstances such as technology, economics, and social attitudes.

Deviant behavior is any conduct that is in conflict with the values and norms of the culture within which the behavior occurs.

Discrimination is the unequal treatment, or mistreatment, of another because of their status such as, but not limited to, race, religion, color, sex, sexual orientation, national origin, age, disability, socioeconomic status, or subculture status. It is illegal to discriminate against specified classes, but unfair discrimination against people outside those classes is legal, even though morally unjustified. Discrimination has to do with behavior while the status of being racist or prejudiced has to do with how one feels and believes irrespective of how they actually treat other people.

Discriminatory behavior can be either negative or positive. For example, an employer may favor hiring members of one class over another and, hence, their discriminatory behavior benefits members of the favored class. But, to what extent favoring a certain class results in unfair discrimination against another depends upon the circumstances. The employer who, when all things are equal, favors hiring Asians, cannot be said to be doing wrong. However, if that employer hires a less qualified Asian over a better qualified non-Asian, because of prejudicial feelings, they are practicing negative discrimination. The police officer who issues a citation to a Black person for speeding ten miles per hour over the limit cannot be said to have issued the citation because the violator was Black, unless that same officer neglects to cite non-Blacks for the same offense.

Ethnocentrism is the belief that one's own culture is superior to that of others and results from the tendency to evaluate others on the basis of the norms of one's own culture. While ethnocentrism is often regarded as being wrong, it is not necessarily so, and for many cultures ethnocentrism is all that has kept them from becoming extinct. To each person, the norms and values of their own culture seem normal and, therefore, right. Accordingly, the norms and values of a different culture can appear, by comparison, to be abnormal and therefore aberrant or wrong.

That cultures collide is not surprising inasmuch as each features a different set of values and practices, and people tend to resent and resist that which they view as different and therefore aberrant, or as a display of nonconformity. For example, it has been observed that some U.S. hosts have criticized their European guests for not practicing proper hygiene. However, American's attending school in Europe have been rebuked for their compulsive preoccupation with hygiene being told it is not necessary to bath every day. Have Americans taken personal hygiene to a level that could be described as obsessive-compulsive, or are the citizens of some European countries derelict in their hygiene? If the members of two different cultures do not agree on what constitutes proper hygiene, why would they be likely to agree on issues of greater importance and consequence? When another culture (or subculture) is regarded as being aberrant or inferior, it is easy to begin the process of stereotyping and scapegoating which in turn can lead to discrimination and persecution.

Genocide is the systematic institutionalized execution (murder) of the members of some specific group whether it is based on religion, race, ethnicity, etc.

Labeling is generally applied to a known individual, as opposed to stereotyping which is generally applied to a group whose members are not known. But, the line of distinction is fine. While labeling can be positive, it is usually negative. But, even positive labels can be detrimental. Asians are labeled and stereotyped as being high academic achievers, imposing an uncomfortable standard against which each individual Asian student is measured. That can present a dilemma for the Asian student whose academic ability is only average.

Oppression can be defined as the keeping down of a person or class by the cruel, overbearing, and unjust use of power or authority; the burdening of someone with harsh and rigorous impositions. It is the act of tyrannizing over someone. Laws can be oppressive, and the manner in which laws are enforced can be oppressive.

Outsiders are those who for various reasons function outside the boundaries of mainstream society. Generally, members of the mainstream society relegate people to the status of outsider because they are for some reason perceived to be different and therefore aberrant.

Persecution occurs when someone subjects another person or class of people to circumstances intended to harass, injure, distress, trouble or annoy constantly, or oppress cruelly. Persecution is often perpetrated for reasons of race, religion, politics, subculture status, sexual preference, etc.

Prejudice is a negative preconceived belief (prejudgment) about a particular person or group that is based little on fact, and views are not subject to change in light of contradictory facts whether they are in the form of verifiably accurate information or experience. The old saying, "I know what I want to believe, don't confuse me with facts," applies here very well.

We have been taught to believe that it is wrong to be prejudiced, but everyone is prejudiced to varying degrees about certain things. We all view things, and feel about things, based on our early life programming process and subsequent life experiences. Hence, everyone feels differently about a variety of issues. If one were socialized in a manner that left them biased or prejudiced about a certain group, that is not the problem. The problem appears when they choose to treat members of the group poorly because of how they feel about them. It could be argued that disliking someone is not wrong, but mistreating him or her is wrong.

Projection is the act of unconsciously attributing one's own negative thoughts, feelings, and behavior, onto another person. An example would be the husband who is cheating on his wife and, although he has no reason to suspect that she is cheating on him, begins to accuse her of being unfaithful. Racist discrimination and persecution can result because of projection. For example, many of the undesirable qualities that Hitler attributed to the Jews were characteristics he himself was guilty of. Adolf Hitler was the leader of the Nazis and chancellor of Germany between the years 1933–1945.

Racism is similar to ethnocentrism in that it is characterized by the belief that one's own race or ethnic group is superior to that of another. Racism often underlies the belief that any unequal treatment, or mistreatment, of the "inferior" group or its members is justified. Whether a person is racist, or not, is not determined so much by their level of formal education but seems to be rooted in a multitude of other factors which includes their own level of self-esteem. Often, how a person perceives others is influenced a great deal by how they view themselves.

Repression is the act of putting down and keeping down, holding back, subduing, restraining, or preventing, the natural development or expression of another person or group. To repress is to control too strictly or severely. Repression is similar to, but not synonymous with, oppression and persecution.

Scapegoating is the blaming of another person, or group, for one's own problems. Adolf Hitler ambitiously blamed the Jews for many of Germany's economic and social ills, broadcast propaganda campaigns accordingly, and the Holocaust ensued. But, Hitler did not just anni-hilate the Jews for his campaign of genocidal extermination targeted also Gypsies, homosexuals, elderly, and the mentally and physically handicapped. Millions were murdered.

Classes of people who live on the fringes of mainstream society have always been convenient scapegoats and have tended to suffer blame when something detrimental occurred while they were in the area. When members of the dominant populous makes a scapegoat of a peripheral group, accusing them of various forms of wrongdoing, that tends to serve as a prelude to later official and legal persecution.

Self-Fulfilling Prophesy is a prediction or treatment that causes a per-son to respond in a certain manner. A self-fulfilling prophesy often occurs when the subject of one or more labels behaves in a manner that conforms to the expectations that the labels imply. For example, a person decides that they don't like another and proceeds to treat that person accordingly. The person being treated in a disparaging man-ner predictably reacts in a negative way. The first person then uses the negative reaction as verification that they were correct in their initial negative assessment of that person.

When a class of people is subjected to chronic discrimination and persecution, the self-fulfilling prophecy concept suggests that their behavior will to varying degrees be fashioned accordingly. Similarly, when a person is frequently the subject of discrimination and/or per-secution, whether on the basis of race, culture, or some other factor, it is easy to understand why they would begin feeling they are being sub-jected to discrimination and/or persecution even when not being so subjected.

Stereotyping can be said to be the application of a rigid, inaccurate, and oversimplified, set of attributes to all members of an entire group.

While stereotyping can be either positive or negative, it is usually negative and especially prevalent relative to those who are perceived to be outsiders such as minorities and members of subculture groups. Stereotyping generally results in distortions of reality inasmuch as it tends to:

1. Overemphasize the extent to which the members of a group are different from the rest of societies members.
2. Fail to acknowledge the extent to which the members of the stereotyped group are similar to the other members of society.
3. Emphasize the extent to which the individual members of a group are alike one with another.
4. Fail to acknowledge the differences that exist between individual members of a group.

Stereotypes, therefore, tend to be misleading because the members of most cultures and subcultures are generally more alike, and less unlike, the members of the mainstream than is generally thought to be the case.

One reason stereotypes endure is that very often they contain an element of truth regardless of its nature or extent. When a stereotype contains an element of truth, even if it is an insignificant element that cannot be applied to the target group as a whole, it is easy to perceive an application even though not justified.

Significantly, the stereotypes that are applied to one class of people can generally be substituted for another with little variation. So, while the cultural characteristics of various outsider groups will vary, the response to them by the members of settled society tends to be predictable and varies only slightly. Hence, to a significant degree, one stereotype fits all!

Who Discriminates?

Minorities, in a position of power, are no less inclined than anyone else to discriminate. In the final analysis, one must realize that we are all human beings and share the failings that accompany such a status.

When contemplating the issue of unfair discrimination, one most commonly thinks of a white person in a position of power discriminating against minorities in one manner or another. However, White people have no monopoly on discrimination and virtually anyone in a position of power and control is a candidate for such behavior.

Historically, in the U.S., many job classifications were closed to women, and women tended to be paid less than men when performing the same job. Increasingly that situation has been changing because of persistent efforts by women to achieve equality. But, while historically women have been discriminated against, many will themselves discriminate once in a position of power. Hence, as with many things, the problem goes both ways. There are many cases wherein a woman in a position of power is conspicuous in her biased hiring and promotional decisions, and treatment of subordinates, favoring women over men.

Related to the issue of discrimination based on sex is the issue of sexual harassment in the work place. It is not uncommon for men to subject women to sexual harassment in the workplace, but women in superior positions have also subjected men to sexual harassment. This writer once observed a female manager, who was unaware anyone was watching, stop beside the desk of a male subordinate and lewdly raise her dress to near waist height and begin adjusting her under garments. That manager was notorious in her mistreatment of male subordinates. When asked how he felt about her indecent display he stated he was offended feeling that she was taunting him. When asked why he did not report the incident he stated that he feared so doing would result in his termination; he was a minority, he knew she would deny the allegation and be believed over him, and the human resource manager was a woman. He said it would be best to say nothing. True, that is but one example, but cases of sexual harassment, perpetrated against men by women in a superior position, in the workplace, does occur. And, if women feel they have little or no recourse when subjected to sexual harassment, men tend to feel the same.

Just as gender, being male versus female, is often a basis for discrimination, so is sexual preference or orientation. It is a fact that homosexuals are often discriminated against relative to employment, often being denied a job because of their sexual preference, or fired once their homosexuality is discovered. Having been hired, many are discriminated against relative to promotions, pay increases, and job assignments, with many also being persecuted by coworkers and supervisors. However, the problem works both ways. There are many cases wherein homosexuals who have achieved a position of authority discriminate just as badly against subordinates because they are heterosexual. It is not uncommon for a homosexual in a position of authority to base hiring decisions on an applicant's sexual orientation, and award promotions, pay increases, and job assignments, using the same criteria. It is also a fact that homosexual supervisors, managers, and co-workers, will sometimes persecute heterosexual employees just as ambitiously as homosexuals are often persecuted. As stated, it goes both ways.

Minorities, in a position of power, are no less inclined than anyone else to discriminate. In the final analysis, one must realize that we are all human beings and share the failings that accompany such a status.

Is All Discrimination Unfair?

In all the examples cited . . . there was a reasonable distinction that rendered the discrimination legitimate and therefore legal.

The word discrimination carries with it many negative connotations and we have been programmed to believe that all forms of discrimination are wrong, but that is not true. Discrimination can be defined as unfair treatment, and/or refusal of normal human rights to people because of such qualities as race, age, sex, nationality, cultural status, or religion. Discrimination is a refusal to treat all people equal where no reasonable distincion between them exists. Note the term *reasonable distinction* and consider it relative to how race may or may not be a legitimate factor when law enforcement practices criminal profiling (discussed in Chapter 2).

As previously stated, while the very nature of profiling is discriminatory, it is not wrong when done for a legitimate purpose and it does not violate constitutionally protected rights. But, when profiling becomes the means, in whole or in part, to execute one or more acts of *unfair* discrimination, or persecution, it is wrong. Note that the word "unfair" was italicized.

Profile can be defined as a short but descriptive biography describing the most outstanding characteristics of a subject That being true, profiling and therefore discrimination is not inherently an unjust practice; it's a question of motive, application, relevance, and the extent to which a reasonable distinction can be demonstrated. For example, the process of insurance rate making is highly discriminatory, but the courts have ruled that insurance companies (relative to premiums) may discriminate, but they may not discriminate unfairly. Smokers being required to pay more for life and health insurance than non-smokers is discriminatory, but the courts have ruled that it does not constitute unfair discrimination because it can be justified by medical research verifying that as a group smokers develop more health problems than non-smokers. A person's age greatly impacts the cost of life insurance; old people buying life insurance pay a higher premium than a young person purchasing the same coverage. That is a case of age discrimination, but it does not constitute unfair discrimination because as a group old people will die sooner than young people. When purchasing automobile insurance, one will note that the rates are not uniform from one state to another, from one city to another, and from one neighborhood to another. The disparity in rates is very discriminatory, but it is not regarded (legally) as being unfairly discriminatory because the differences are based on provable factors such as the accident and theft rates in various areas, as well as the cost of repairs.

In all the examples cited above there was a reasonable distinction that rendered the discrimination legitimate and therefore legal. Reflect back to Chapter 2, "Criminal Profiling (Police Profiling Practices)," and consider the degree to which reasonable distinction renders the inclusion of race and national origin among profiling criteria legitimate.

What Constitutes Deviant Behavior?

But, because other cultures operating in proximity to the dominant society have their own norms, differences exist that can be interpreted as being deviant and result in conflict.

People are generally discriminated against because they feature one or more characteristics that make them "different" from the norm and they are therefore perceived to be deviant. Deviant behavior can be defined as any behavior that is inconsistent with the norms and values of the culture within which it occurs irrespective of whether the behavior is legal or illegal. For example, in the U.S., urinating in the street publicly would be regarded as deviant behavior, yet in some cultures so doing is an accepted practice. In American culture it is an accepted practice to endearingly pat someone on the back or even pat the top of his or her head. However, in Asian cultures, patting someone on the head is a serious insult. American men do not walk about holding hands, but in some cultures, such as in Saudi Arabia, it is done with no homosexual implications. Drug use, in America, although illegal is not regarded by many people as representing deviant behavior and that, in part, is why the drug problem is as acute as it is today.

The norms and values of a culture do not normally present a problem so long as all the members honor them within accepted parameters. The problem results when someone deviates from the accepted norms. America, being a mosaic of cultures, and subcultures, features a plethora of diverging values and norms, but there is a reasonably well defined set of general values and norms that are embraced by the majority and expected to be honored by all. But, because other cultures operating in proximity to the dominant society have their own norms, differences exist that can be interpreted as being deviant and result in conflict.

When norms are violated, consequences can result. In many cases it is the violator who suffers the consequences. However, there are cases where the consequences are suffered by the one whose norms were violated. For example, some years ago police with a search warrant raided the home of a Gypsy family, and while conducting their search male officers put their hands in the dress pockets of the women. In that culture, married women who are touched by another man become unclean leaving them outcasts within their culture. That they were unwilling victims of such a violation does not mitigate the seriousness of the situation and they will remain outcasts. At the time of the raid, almost certainly, the police officers conducting the search did not understand the cultural significance of what they were doing to the women by putting their hands in their pockets, and the devastating lifelong consequences the women would suffer as a result. It would have been acceptable had female officers conducted the search of the women.

Does Society Create Outsiders?

Hence, mainstream society attempts to maintain itself by excluding those who are perceived to be deviant, or transform them into the mainstream social structure through an acculturation process.

Accepting that deviant behavior is any behavior that is inconsistent with the norms and values of the culture within which it occurs, there is justification for asserting that it is society that creates outsiders. For the most part the dominant society has a set of values, a social structure that is embraced by its members within accepted parameters with ambiguity being unacceptable; there is a status quo that must not be upset or challenged. Those who do not conform are labeled as deviant and relegated to the status of outsider. The consequence of being labeled deviant is that those who are labeled as such are cut off from the rest of society. That takes the form of social exclusion, repressive legislation, and also commonly in the form of discrimination in education, housing, and employment. In some cases overt persecution occurs. An example of exclusion is bikers being prohibited from attending classical music performances at the Center for the Arts in one of America's larger cities. The bikers did not choose to stay away, but were arbitrarily excluded. "Groups are identified as outsiders because their social structures and economies are perceptibly different from those of the larger society. They are peripheral in the sense that there is a considerable social distance between them and the majority—there is little or no social interaction—and this social gulf is usually, but not necessarily, reinforced by spatial separation" (Sibley, 1981).

In most cases the barriers that exist between members of the dominant society and members of outsider groups are created and perpetuated by the dominant society more so than by the outsider groups whether they be cultures or subcultures, as discussed above. "Social groups create deviance by making the rules whose infraction constitutes deviance by applying these rules to particular people and labeling them as outsiders" (Plummer, 1979). While admittedly those who belong to outsider groups do practice an alternative lifestyle, and embrace a value system that is in some respects different from that of the dominant society, that does not justify the assertion that they have chosen to be outsiders. There is a difference between choosing exclusion, and suffering exclusion. In the final analysis, it is societies intolerant response to those who are different that makes them outsiders; they become outsiders by being cut off from the rest of society.

Some will argue that members of peripheral groups make themselves outsiders by deviating from mainstream norms, and if they don't like the resultant exclusion they should change and conform to mainstream values. Such an argument serves as evidence of the climate of intolerance being referred to, and it validates the assertion that society creates outsiders; it is societies intolerance for anything that deviates from what they consider to be proper that creates outsiders.

Outsider groups, having been labeled as deviant, are not likely to change in response to the label, and "increased deviance" generally does not occur, because they do not view themselves as being deviant. And, while outsider groups generally do not view the values of the mainstream as being deviant even though different from their own, the members of the mainstream very much view the values of outsider groups as being deviant. Their view of the outsider group as being deviant ignores the fact that the outsiders embrace most of the general values of mainstream society, but focuses on those things that are different.

Further, while outsiders do not tend to impose their values onto the members of the dominant society in a way that encourages change on their part, the members of the dominant society do impose their values on the members of outsider groups and, if outsiders are to be accepted, or at least tolerated, they must mimic the values of the dominant society. Hence, mainstream society attempts to maintain itself by excluding those who are perceived to be deviant, or transform them into the mainstream social structure through an acculturation process.

If it is true that society creates deviance, which leads to the designation of outsiders, which in turn leads to discrimination and persecution of those labeled as deviant outsiders, we have a set of cyclic dynamics germane to the issue of discrimination, a self-fulfilling prophesy worthy of analysis.

Chapter 6

CULTURAL AWARENESS

This discussion, if it serves no other purpose, will leave the reader aware of how cryptic and elusive some cultures and subcultures can be, and why efforts to study them almost always end in varying degrees of frustration.

Introduction

Cultural awareness is prerequisite to understanding many aspects of the issues of profiling and discrimination. And, although racial profiling is a much publicized cliché, and commonly thought of as being a law enforcement issue, it should be apparent to the reader at this point that it is more a social issue. Accordingly, courses in psychology and sociology on the community college or university level are highly recommended.

Many very good sociological studies have been done and the writers have never ceased to be amazed at the ability of sociologists to study a variety of groups that in many respects represent a notable departure from the culture of the social scientific researcher. In spite of the fact that the social researcher often begins a study being at a conspicuous disadvantage, the results are generally very good and provide valuable information and insight. However, some studies are left with informational deficits because some cultures and subcultures are so cryptic and elusive as to defy reliable study.

The following is provided to enhance cultural awareness, and to illuminate a few of the mentioned informational deficits and the reasons for them. This discussion, if it serves no other purpose, will leave the reader aware of how cryptic and elusive some cultures and subcultures can be, and why efforts to study them almost always end in varying

degrees of frustration. Those chosen for examination are very prevalent in American society, but poorly understood, and they are the targets of notable discrimination, persecution, and stereotyping, and the
subject of enduring myths.

It is hoped this discussion will stimulate a resolution for further
study of sociology, but the reader should approach any academic treatise on the groups mentioned with measured skepticism. The author
has noted that much of the literature focusing on some cultures and
subcultures is very reliable while some simply perpetuate earlier writings with the information therefore badly dated and/or inaccurate. An
unfortunate consequence of that is the often resultant tendency to perpetuate inaccurate information, prevailing stereotypes, and myths.
That tendency manifests itself very much relative to bikers (subculture) and Gypsies (culture) whose individual members are not all alike
any more than are the individuals within any other cultural group.
Those two groups have been chosen for brief examination here for
several reasons.

1. They are so cryptic and elusive as to defy reliable study.
2. They are very prevalent in America.
3. They are badly misunderstood and the subject of many enduring
   stereotypes and myth.
4. They have suffered a history of discrimination, persecution, and
   repressive legislation.
5. They illustrate so well the discrepancy that so often exists between
   stereotype and fact.
6. They tend to be overlooked when discussing cultural awareness
   and sensitivity, and much of the information that is disseminated
   about them is inaccurate. Discussing them has merit because they
   feature some valuable sociological uniqueness that well illustrates
   many of the points made throughout this book, and discussing
   them helps to avoid conforming to what may be regarded as a traditional view of the topics.

When reading this section the reader should keep in mind that
many generalizations are being presented and not everyone within
any group feels the same about various issues. Readers should also
understand that when discussing the fear that some people have of the
police, generalizations are again being made and there is no intention

to malign police officers. Some years ago the news commentator, Paul Harvey, stated that studies have shown that relative to ethics and integrity police officers have demonstrated a better performance record than the clergy. In any group there will always be the few proverbial rotten apples and, unfortunately, the police are no exception. It has been said that people fear the power that the police have, but it would be more accurate to say that they fear the potential misuse of that power.

Why Some Classes Are Resistant to Social Scientific Study

Cultures and subcultures to varying degrees feature an internal order that is well hidden and won't be revealed.

What is discussed here relative to the inability of sociologists to effectively study some of the more cryptic cultures and subcultures is not meant to minimize them, for the shortcomings are those things that they themselves acknowledge.

As stated, many cultures and subcultures defy reliable academic study, and there are several reasons for that. In many cases the target group will not make the disclosures necessary for a reliable view into their inner world, their culture and economies. And, the task of studying them is badly complicated by the fact that the culture will feature both visible and hidden elements that render any analysis ambiguous. Accordingly, the study will tend to be distracted by the visible elements while the hidden elements remain undetected. Cultures and subcultures to varying degrees feature an internal order that is well hidden and won't be revealed. In many cases the subjects of the study will manipulate the study not only by withholding information, but also by providing misinformation, a task that is simplified by the fact that there are both visible and hidden elements of the culture or subculture, and prevailing stereotypes can be used to advantage when thwarting a study. The subjects of many studies have an incentive to manipulate the study because they know that the researchers intention is to later publish his or her findings. The incentive to manipulate a study is especially strong if experience has demonstrated that anonymity is fundamental to avoiding discrimination and persecution. It is difficult to manipulate, dominate, and control, a class whose intricate interworkings are poorly understood, with that being especially true when the government is largely unaware of their existence.

Those who endeavor to study certain groups are almost always members of mainstream society and that renders them less able to realize results on anything but a superficial level. That occurs because the researcher is to varying degrees impeded by a mainstream frame of reference that limits insight and depth of analysis. When attempting to study a group that is cryptic and whose members are resistant to being studied it is difficult to separate fact from fiction without an adequate initial understanding of the target group and, relative to certain groups, an adequate initial understanding is almost never the case.

Bias as well as assumptions on the part of the researcher can diminish the reliability of a study. Those who are biased risk forming a premature hypothesis and then going in search of supporting facts while dismissing information that contradicts their initial hypothesis. Similar to that is the unfortunate tendency of the academic community to expect things to fit within a categorical framework that is accepted as constituting the foundation of acceptable knowledge; things must fit into, and be consistent with, established and accepted models. Also, the academician's often conformist tendencies can hinder attempts to study outsider groups, those groups that are on the fringes of the dominant society; the academician does not want to be viewed by colleagues as an academic heretic. The underlying motive of the researcher can also affect the reliability of results. Most researchers do a commendable job in their quest to determine facts and are equally candid about that which they were unable to accomplish. Others, it would appear, are less interested in fact than in eventually being congratulated by academic colleagues for their subsequent literary masterpiece. In the academic community there is an understanding that one must "publish or perish." Scholars in the academic community are expected to be published. Finally, some it would seem are more interested in the marketability of their published results.

Academicians are also limited in what they can learn about some cultures and subcultures by virtue of their being unable or unwilling to live within a culture for the extended period that would be necessary. By "extended" is meant many years. To be sure, a non-Gypsy (gauje) could not study that culture by becoming a part of it. But, how about bikers or hoboes for example? Those two groups are not cultures but, rather, subcultures. Many mainstream people own and ride Harley-

Davidson motorcycles, and they "rub elbows" with real bikers. By so doing they obtain a glimpse into that subculture. But, even though they may be known and liked by bikers, the bikers will permit only a limited view into their inner world and, also, even if not withheld many of the subtleties go unnoticed.

Study of hoboes is almost always done from a distance. The sociologist who studies them does not become absorbed into that lifestyle for the extended period necessary to become a part of that harsh world. And, even if they did, many of the subtleties would escape them for they do not share a common frame of reference and corresponding values. The sociologist was not driven into that world by life circumstances, but chose to enter it for purposes of study. Hence, though not physically distanced they are psychologically and socially distanced. At no time during the study do they view themselves as a hobo and neither do they think and feel as a hobo. They remain an academician "tagging along" so as to study them.

If the social scientist assumes the indigent lifestyle they do so knowing that they can leave it whenever they so desire and, in fact, will be leaving it. And, during the study they retain their ties to their mainstream reference group of family, friends, and professional colleagues. If they encounter problems with police and storeowners they know it is because of what they appear to be, the role they have willingly but temporarily assumed as an academician, not because of what and who they really are. There is a difference between being poor and pretending to be poor. The two do not feel the same. The people they are amongst during the study are generally poorly educated with limited opportunity to rise above their station. Conversely, the sociologist is well educated and can leave that world at any time, and during their excursion into the world of their subjects they have finances supporting them that the subjects do not have. They are not destitute.

Some years ago a female news reporter endeavored to live among the homeless to study them "from the inside" intending to prepare a news story about them and their lives. She aborted the effort after just one day stating that their world was simply too harsh. Had she endured she would have learned a lot, to be sure, but it would still have been a study from a distance, not from a spatial distance but from a psychological and social distance; she was not homeless. She was not a part of their world any more than they were a part of her's. She could feel sympathy for them but never feel despair in the way they do or experience their brand of camaraderie. Accepting that her feelings towards the target group were sympathetic, and granting that her motives for the intended study were well intended, her view of the homeless could be little more than condescending. Almost certainly she was unaware of how quickly the subjects of her study would detect that.

The following information does not even scratch the surface but is intended to stimulate insight and illustrate the importance of understanding how complex and poorly understood many cultures and subcultures can be. The following is intended to provide insight while carefully avoiding the divulging of information that the groups in question would not wish to have divulged. Aside from briefly discussing common "core values" of various cultures, for the purpose of offering insight, this discussion proceeds to hoboes, tramps, bums, and the homeless. Following that, this examination addresses bikers, a highly visible subculture, and Gypsies, an extremely cryptic and invisible culture. Those two groups have been chosen for reasons already stated.

Cultural "Core Value" Highlights

African-American's display a strong kinship to extended family, strong religious convictions, and prioritize education as a social strength. Significantly, among law enforcement personnel, there are more Blacks (8.6%) with graduate degrees than Hispanics (5.2%) and Whites (3.7%) (Hennessy, 2000).

Asians have core values that while similar will vary depending upon the nationality in question whether it be Chinese, Korean, Japanese, Thai, Vietnamese, etc. But, generally speaking, it can be said that cooperation and harmony is emphasized while competition is discouraged. They have a sense of group unity with individual contributions to the group tending to be more important than individual interests (Hennessy, 2000). Educational achievement is strongly emphasized from the time of birth. With Asians, more than with many other cultures, being able to save face (avoid humiliation–retain dignity) when dealing with adversity is vitally important.

Hispano-Latino cultures include Mexicans, Puerto Ricans, Cubans, South Americans, and Central Americans. In those cultures high value is placed on honor of family and personal reputation. Extended family is very important and theirs is a very patriarchal culture (Law

Enforcement Television, 1993). Machismo is a characteristic requiring that the male not be humiliated in the presence of others. For example, it would be an insult to make negative statements, to the male, reflecting on a female family member. Contrary to the stereotype suggesting laziness, they have a strong work ethic.

Arab-Americans are very devoted to family and business with respect being acquired by their success in those areas. It is a very patriarchal culture although both men and women are highly valued. Religion and language are important with adherence to many old world beliefs. (Law Enforcement Television, 1993). Not everyone living in the Arab world is Arab; there are other ethnic and racial groups such as Kurds, Druze, Copts, Assyrians, Armenians, and Berbers. The Arab world encompasses an array of ethnic, racial, linguistic, and religious groups. The Arab macro cultures are pluralistic in nature and are increasingly multicultural (Hennessy, 2000).

Subculture Groups
(Hoboes, Tramps, Bums, & Homeless)

> *The difficulty of identification results from the fact that while each will usually function within the category to which they most accurately belong, many will at times practice the lifestyle of another.*

Most people have heard the terms hobo, tramp, and bum, and often the terms are used interchangeably as if they were synonymous one with the other. In truth, however, they are each a distinct group even though it is not always easy to distinguish one from the other without knowing more about the individuals long term history and lifestyle.

The difficulty of identification results from the fact that while each will usually function within the category to which they most accurately belong, many will at times practice the lifestyle of another. That will be discussed more fully. In its truest form the hobo is a migratory worker while the tramp is a migratory non-worker. The bum does not work and neither is he migratory. The hobo, although being a migratory worker, will commonly go for extended periods without working and therefore can appear to be a tramp or at times even a bum. Conversely, one may find a tramp working although not often. It is common for a tramp and bum to frequent inner city rescue missions for food, shower, and a bed, a practice that is looked down upon by the hobo who refers to them, disdainfully, as mission stiffs. However, many a hobo will on occasion avail himself to the services of a rescue mission but the difference is, so far as they are concerned, the fact they are not dependent upon the missions as they consider the former to be.

As for the assertion that the tramp is a migratory non-worker, there are hoboes who will argue that the tramp does work (as do the hoboes) but differentiate them from the hobo subculture more on the basis of the fact that the tramp does not ride the trains as was historically characteristic of the hobo, but walks and hitchhikes everywhere he goes. And, the tramp tends to be more solitary than the hobo and is also socially distanced from the hobo—two different subculture groups. Again, we see factors that complicate the effort to determine to what subculture group an individual most accurately belongs.

Historically the hobo subculture was well defined with very definite rules of the road, rules of etiquette and expected behavior that were taught by the group and enforced by the group. The rules served to ensure harmony among the members and prevent conflict with those in settled society. Rules consisted of such things as when in town, do not speak with the women; when knocking on the door of a home seeking food, go to the back door, not the front; when asking for food, offer to work for it; do not solicit money or food from another hobo; when using a jungle (hobo camp) leave it as found for the next person; it is acceptable to ask another hobo where they are going but not where they are coming from; when one or more hoboes are at a jungle fire (camp fire) one may not approach them and their fire but, rather, must speak with them from a distance and approach only when invited to do so.

The well-defined and honored rules of the road as known and practiced by the old timers are largely gone owing to the number of younger people now on the road who suffer psychiatric and substance abuse problems, with many being criminals on the lam (fugitives). Some will argue that few real hoboes are left because today few are riding the trains (freight trains). Accepting that the hobo is a migratory worker, one must recognize that they still exist, in large numbers, even though they have changed with the times. There are some who feel that to be a true hobo one must ride the trains because historically they did. However, riding the trains had nothing to do with being a migratory worker; they rode the trains because they needed transportation and the trains were there to be ridden, at no cost.

Today there are not many hoboes riding the trains for several reasons. First, because of drugs and crime it is too dangerous to be riding the trains. Second, the anatomy of a train has changed to where riding them is no longer easy. The boxcars are now rarely left open when empty, and containerized shipments and piggybacks have eliminated many of the boxcars. Third, there are notably fewer rail miles today. Fourth, the railroad police remain an obstacle. Many wannabe hoboes (hobby hoboes) who ride the trains for sport have made matters worse for the true hobo, the migratory worker who relied upon the trains for transportation. While railroad workers and railroad police would often look the other way when a real hobo was at issue, they cannot afford to do so with the sport rider. The real hobo knew how to jump the trains in a reasonably safe manner and if they did get hurt they did not sue the railroad. That is not true of the sport rider. Hence, the railroads have intensified enforcement efforts. Also, railroad authorities knew that the real hobo would not vandalize and steal railroad property for the same reason they left the women alone when in town. Unfortunately, today, theft and vandalism on railroad property is a serious problem.

During those years that the boes did ride the trains, they did not always ride them. For example, the hobo going to Wenatchee, Washington, to pick fruit (apple knockers) would ride the trains there. But, once harvest was over and they had been paid, they purchased a bus or train ticket to leave town to avoid the jack-rollers who would be waiting along the way to rob them. Also, when harvest was pending and labor was needed, the railroad police along the train routes leading to Wenatchee tended to be lenient, but not so once harvest had been completed and hobo labor was no longer needed. Today, the migratory worker hitchhikes (illegal in some states) buys a bus ticket, or drives a car, the latter referred to in their culture as rubber tramps or rubber tire hoboes.

A note of historical interest: Many have heard of the legendary markings that hoboes would leave to let other hoboes know such things as what town had hostile police officers, what house was good for a food hand out, etc. Such markings appear to have existed in legend only. The author has never seen such markings and has been told by old hoboes that they have never seen such markings, the old timers having hoboed during the 1930s. It is difficult to believe that such markings were used if the old timers are unfamiliar with them. If they were ever used, they likely were used by army veterans who took to the road hoboing at the end of the Civil War, but that is not a theory being proposed by the writers.

Hoboes vary in the territory they cover. Some confine their travels to one or a few states while others will range a considerable distance. Many hoboes go by a road name with their real name generally being unknown to others. Hoboes and bikers have road names as opposed to prostitutes and criminals who have street names. It is not uncommon for hoboes and bikers to know someone for years only by their road name never knowing, or even wondering, what their real name is. Mainstream people generally would not understand that phenomenon feeling that it would be natural to want to know the persons real name but, to the hobo or biker, it's irrelevant. Hoboes, although they have permanent place of residence, do not consider themselves to be homeless.

Historically the term bum has been applied to what is thought of as a skid row alcoholic, a homeless vagrant or derelict. Loosely applied that definition still holds true with drugs added to the substance abuse inventory. It would be accurate to say that virtually all bums are homeless, but not all homeless are bums. Who will be found represented among the homeless will vary depending on who does the study, the purpose of the study, when the study is done, how the study is done, where the study is done, the economic situation of the area at the time the study is done, and the climatic conditions of the area in which the study is done. The truth of that is reflected in the following percentage figures that do not total 100 percent as one may feel they should. Also, there are many homeless people who satisfy the criteria for more than one category. For example, just because one suffers psychiatric problems does not mean they do not also have a substance abuse problem. Hence, it is not possible to place the people into well-defined categories because the lines separating each are not always clear or absolute. Therefore, the following figures provide insight only.

35% Alcoholic or some other form of substance abuse.
23% Psychiatric problems.
22% Working a low paying job.
33% Families.

Bikers
(A Subculture)

Having stated that members of minority groups, and subculture groups, fear unfair treatment by the system, it is significant to note that many mainstream people also expect such people to be treated unfairly.

To illustrate how little is often known about other cultures and subcultures, and how misunderstood outsider groups can be, and the enduring nature of stereotypes and myths, consider for a moment a highly visible but badly misunderstood group, bikers. That group is viewed by many as being a disorganized group of antisocial, lawless renegades who favor a certain brand of motorcycle (Harley-Davidson). In truth, it is a well-defined yet extremely varied subculture featuring strata of subcultures with the lines separating each being notably blurred. In fact, it is so socially structured, yet varied, that there would be merit to a full semester college level course on the topic. The problem is, no one outside the subculture would be capable of teaching such a course, and no one within the subculture would be willing to do so. In fact, most people within the subculture understand, for the most part, only the strata of which they are a part. Hence, most people within the subculture would be incapable of teaching such a course even if they were willing to do so.

It was mentioned that it is often difficult to ascertain if someone is a hobo, tramp, or bum without knowing more about the individuals long-term history as it pertains to lifestyle and values. So it is with bikers. There are many who appear to be a biker although in reality they are not, and there are many who look less like a biker than stereotypes suggest, yet they are very much a biker. And, there are those who although not a biker they are more akin to bikers in terms of lifestyle and values than is the case with many people who ride. To ascertain if someone is a biker one must be cognizant of the lines separating the biker from the motorcycle enthusiast for the criteria extends far beyond an affinity for Harley-Davidson motorcycles. It has to do with values and norms for there is a notable difference between a biker and a motorcycle enthusiast.

Admittedly, just as is the case with many cultures and subcultures, there is a criminal element among bikers referred to by subculture members as "one percenters" meaning that probably no more than one percent of their people are criminal in nature. The number is certainly greater than one percent, but the point is that the number of criminals among them almost certainly is no greater than exists in settled society. The citizen's tend to refer to one percenters as outlaw bikers. Some one percenter clubs, if they have a criminal agenda, are in every sense of the word a secret society with some having intruded into the arena of organized crime.

There is a system of values, a code of ethics and etiquette, among bikers that while admittedly different from those embraced by members of mainstream society, they tend to be more intact. However, the code of ethics will vary by strata. For example, there was a case where two houses, one across the street from the other, were occupied by bikers. One group was criminal while the other was not. There was no social interaction between the two groups. However, by their appearance it would have been impossible to distinguish one group from the other.

Relative to the assertion that there is a system of values among bikers that although different from those of settled society they tend to be more intact, that is in keeping with what is referred to by some sociologists as value stretch, discussed earlier.

Many people believe that bikers don't work, a stereotype not based on fact. Biker's hold many types of jobs both blue and white collar, both civilian and governmental. Many own their own businesses. As a group they tend to be very well traveled, street smart, and cosmopolitan in their views. They also have their own clergy to officiate worship services, weddings, and funerals. There are many bikers who are as devoutly religious as any mainstream churchgoer, a fact that is not consistent with the negative stereotypes and labels that have been applied to them.

Like Gypsies, many bikers (male and female) have learned to be chameleons to avoid job discrimination. Many corporate executives are unaware of the number of bikers in their work force groomed and wearing clothing selected to conceal their subculture status. Another stereotype is that bikers share their women who are passed about within the group. The truth is they don't. In fact, they often tend to respect their women more than is found in settled society, at least in certain strata. Another stereotype is that drug use among bikers is heavy. In fact, the extent of drug use among them is no greater than will be found in settled society. It was stated that there is a varied social strata among bikers and those who are into drug use and drug sales will generally be found in a certain strata, one mentioned previously. One biker, who is adamantly opposed to illicit drug use commented on the number of times someone has attempted to purchase drugs from him assuming that because he is a biker he must have and be selling drugs.

It is not uncommon for culturally displaced individuals to find a niche in the biker subculture because they are a group that will accept them without bias when members of settled society will not. If there is a language barrier bikers will take the time to listen, and if they are culturally different, that difference tends to be regarded simply as a cultural difference and not an indication that they are a lesser person to be shunned. One biker's wife commented that her husband being part American Indian, part Hispanic, and part white, has had difficulty on jobs because socially many of the members of any of the respective groups do not accept him. It is not surprising that he found a social niche with bikers where his ethnicity is not an issue; no one cares. That situation is significant when viewed in light of the assertion that society creates outsiders. Some years ago there was a biker club who had a deaf member; the response was that all members learned sign language. A mainstream lady related having been involved in an automobile accident and no one would stop to render aid except for a group of bikers who remained with her until emergency personnel arrived. Unlike many people, they do not have an aversion to getting involved when involvement is warranted.

There are many bikers who are independents meaning they have no club affiliations. Most remain unaffiliated because they simply do not desire club membership while others (a few) are independent because they are antisocial and incapable of conforming to the norms of a club. Some clubs are small and local while some are very large being national and even international in scope. Some are loosely organized while others are highly organized. Large clubs that are well organized have an impressive intelligence gathering capability exceeded only by government. Their members, the member's women, and non-members, who associate with them, hold jobs in nearly all segments of business, industry, and government at various levels. Hence, there is very little information they do not have access to by one means or another.

A factor that has always distinguished organized crime from non-organized crime is the advantages cultivated by corrupting government, political, and judicial officials. Money corrupts and large well-organized clubs, if they have a criminal agenda, are sufficiently funded to exploit such a strategy. To what extent that has occurred this writer does not know and probably no one does except for the top echelon of the organizations that have cultivated such a strategy, if they have.

Some large clubs have a management structure that is as efficient, sometimes more so, than that of a major corporation. One large club, 30 years ago, consisted of various local chapters with little centralized control. Their president, within about a 25 year period of time, transformed the club into a highly cohesive and well structured organization that is now international in scope with a multibillion dollar budget, and it is better organized and managed than many large corporations. There are few Corporate CEOs who could have accomplished what he did, especially considering the maverick nature of the personnel he had to start with; he had the vision, insight, and leadership skills, to accomplish it and he did it well. Like a corporation they have grown through recruitment, acquisitions, and mergers, and in the process ridding themselves of anyone who was felt to be a liability rather than an asset. While the legality of the organization's agenda is questionable, one must stand in awe at what he accomplished.

A schoolteacher, married to a biker, once commented to this writer that she had observed that many bikers have what she considered to be quirks. She seemed to understand when told that many, if not most, grew up in an environment that was to varying degrees on the fringes of the dominant society and, further, being on the fringes of society causes one to become labeled by the dominant society as outsiders thus increasing social distance.

Many bikers feel little reason to trust a society and its governmental representatives feeling they have both demonstrated a propensity for discrimination and persecution. A biker has violated very few mainstream people, but bikers are commonly violated by members of the mainstream via discrimination, persecution, obscene gestures, and aggravated assault using their vehicle.

Having stated that members of minority groups, and subculture groups, fear unfair treatment by the system, it is significant to note that many mainstream people also expect such people to be treated unfairly. The author recalls witnessing an accident wherein two bikers, on motorcycles, ran over a drunk pedestrian who had emerged from between two vehicles. It was surprising the number of mainstream people who witnessed the accident, who would normally have chosen to not get involved, remained at the scene to tell the police what had happened fearing that their failure to do so would result in the bikers being unfairly charged. Among the people who remained were a young mother and an elderly couple. The elderly woman stated that she had told her husband "There was nothing those boys could have done to avoid that accident and if we don't go back and tell the police what we saw they are going to be railroaded!"

Bikers are not a protected class inasmuch as existing laws are intended to provide protection against discrimination based on race, religion, color, sex, national origin, age, and disability. Simply being a biker does not entitle one to protection under the law on the basis of any of those categories although individual members are entitled to protection under the law if they belong to one of the protected categories.

Although bikers are often stereotyped as being violent and lawless, police officers that work in areas featuring both biker bars and non-biker bars report that the frequency and nature of disturbance calls to biker bars versus non-biker bars are no different. Similarly, police officers have observed that there are few disturbances at biker rallies, especially considering the large number of attendees. Yearly more than one quarter million bikers converge on Sturgis, South Dakota, a town of approximately 7,000 population, for a ten day rally yet, as reported by law enforcement, there are significantly few disturbances. They are a very self-policing group.

Daytona Beach, Florida, is the site of a yearly weeklong biker rally and police report having no major problems with them aside from the need for traffic control because of the large number of attendees. The same holds true when the Daytona 500 races take place the previous week; no unusual problems, just a need for traffic control. Citizen complaints that are received by the police department relative to the biker rally are from beach residents regarding excessive noise. Conversely, each year college students go to Daytona Beach on spring break, and Daytona is the site of the yearly Black College Reunion. The Black College Reunion began around 1987 as a college reunion but has evolved into a weekend cruising event. The police report having significant problems with both groups relative to offenses such as drunk and disorderly, fights, urinating and defecating on the beach, public nudity, simulated sex acts, etc. Beach residents are far more troubled by the college students than by the attendees of the races or biker rally.

Why do the police in Daytona Beach have far more problems with the college students (black and white) than they do with bikers? It has to do with age and values. Most bikers are adults seeking to enjoy themselves and desire to be left alone. As for the college students, one is dealing with the impetuousness of youth. When the biker rally occurs in Daytona, there is a strong police presence to serve as a deterrent and for response capability should trouble develop; they are primarily concerned with the criminal element that does exist in the biker subculture, as stated earlier.

A final comment relative to bikers and stereotypes has merit. A few years ago there was a biker event held at a large hotel in a major southwest city. Several of the wait staff told some of the bikers that they were tame and a pleasure to serve stating that when doctors and lawyers hold an event there, they are less courteous and as one employee said, "they tear the place up." Stereotypes would suggest just the opposite.

Gypsies
(A Culture)

It is well known what was done to the Jews during the holocaust, but few people realize that a similar effort to annihilate the Gypsies preceded what was done to the Jews with staggering casualties. Total casualties are unknown but some estimates put the figure at a million or more. Entire villages were decimated yet significantly, and sadly, not a single Gypsy was invited to testify at the Nuremberg trials.

The perception that settled people (mainstream people) have of Gypsies is often a romantic one, but the reality is very different and generally harsh. Gypsies tend to be viewed within the stereotypes that have been applied to them, many of which do contain some element of truth, many were true at one time in history but are no longer valid, and many are untrue and have always been untrue.

Most Gypsies are not musicians and fortune-tellers, but they have a reputation for such because many are, and they tend to be very good at it. Even today there are well known musicians in the entertainment industry who are Gypsies but the listening audience is unaware that they are Gypsies because their heritage is not publicly acknowledged. While it is a fact that historically many Gypsies told fortunes for money, and still do, there are now many non-Gypsies who are telling fortunes for money.

Fortune-tellers, when doing what they refer to as a cold reading, deduce things about a person by observing such things as their style and mannerisms and by being alert to seemingly insignificant but self-disclosing things they say. By way of deductions drawn from such observations, by understanding the human heart well, and by understanding those things that predictably apply to virtually everyone, they can tell the person things about themselves that leaves them astonished and believing such revelations could only have come from a psychic insight; the person must be clairvoyant! Gypsy fortune-tellers are legendary in such ability and remain to this day the best. Accepting that they are the best one must question why for the answer can provide valuable insight. In reality there is no single reason. But, having historically been a people estranged from the settled societies through which they have passed, and on whose fringes they have lived, having been shunned and persecuted, they have learned to read people well as a matter of survival, literally and economically.

It is well known what was done to the Jews during the holocaust, but few people realize that a similar effort to annihilate the Gypsies preceded what was done to the Jews with staggering casualties. Total casualties are unknown but some estimates put the figure at a million or more. Entire villages were decimated yet significantly, and sadly, not a single Gypsy was invited to testify at the Nuremberg trials.

It is a sad commentary that many countries continue to enact repressive legislation specifically targeting the Gypsies. Generally, repressive legislation will be dressed to give it the appearance of legitimacy, for the good of society, with the biased intent and underlying motive obscured. But, sometimes legislation will be drafted in a manner that officially proclaims the target culture to be undesirable. Also, as in the case of Gypsies, they will sometimes be persecuted with the justification being the assertion that they are not "real" Gypsies and therefore not entitled to the legal protection to which a "real" Gypsy would be entitled. That has occurred in Europe where often members of settled society and their lawmakers have had difficulty (allegedly) distinguishing the Gypsy from the Irish Tinker. When officially proclaiming that the Gypsy is entitled to certain rights and protections, but the Tinker is not, it is convenient to allege a difficulty of identification and differentiation.

Often repressive legislation will not specify a target group, but will target specific activities knowing that it will impact the intended people. For example, in some states and cities of the United States there was no law specifying that the Gypsies could not tell fortunes in return for money, but laws were enacted making it illegal for anyone to tell fortunes for money knowing that at the time it was primarily the Gypsies who were telling fortunes; they were the intended target. The same holds true for many of the laws currently in effect in parts of Europe as will be discussed.

There was a time when it was illegal for a Gypsy to reside in some countries, and until 1855, in Moldavia (a former principality and district of Romania) enslaving Gypsies was legal and a slave owner was free to kill a Gypsy slave if he so desired. In Spain it was not until 1959 that Gypsies were declared to have the same judicial rights as the rest of the population. In parts of Europe, officially regarding a nomadic lifestyle and its attendant activities as being aberrant, there continues to be legislation intended to suppress such a lifestyle with the obvious intention of maintaining dominance and forcing conformance.

Gypsies continue to be regarded as thieves without equal, but in Europe where unlike the United States they are more visible, the authorities report that the number of criminals among them is no greater than is found in the general population. Yet, in the United States, when Gypsies are arrested for a crime the authorities and news media are quick to emphasize that those involved were Gypsies but fail to mention nationality when someone else is arrested for a similar crime. That is unfair and unfortunate, yet in part the Gypsies themselves are to blame.

Gypsies have chosen to live a cryptic lifestyle to avoid discrimination and persecution, yet there is a consequence that accompanies such a choice. When the honest and hard working Gypsies are not seen, which is the majority of them, but the criminals among them are seen, it is predictable that the stereotype suggesting all Gypsies are thieves will be reinforced. But, while choosing to live a cryptic life has caused collateral problems, failure to maintain a cryptic posture would leave them the victims of discrimination and persecution.

For Gypsies, job discrimination remains a fact that is painfully evident every time one of them is foolish enough to come out of the proverbial closet. Many a Gypsy has been denied a job because of their heritage, and fired from a job once their heritage was discovered. So, should they continue to remain cryptic to avoid discrimination but suffer the problems accompanying such a choice, or should they come forth and suffer discrimination and persecution? In the final analysis, considering the extent to which they have been, and continue to be, discriminated against and persecuted, remaining cryptic seems to be the better choice, the choice generating fewer consequences.

Communism failed. However, during the time that it was in effect the Gypsies within the Soviet Satellite countries enjoyed a social safety net that minimized the effects of discrimination, and in those countries education and employment were universal. That safety net was lost when communism failed and deep-rooted racial hatreds reemerged and along with it discrimination in education, employment, and housing.

In the Czech Republic there is an effort to construct 15-foot high walls to segregate Gypsy occupied apartments from the homes of non-Gypsies. The Gypsies and Czech human rights groups have argued that it is an attempt to create ghettos and an example of officially designating the Gypsies as outsiders. Those favoring the construction of walls argue that Gypsies are undesirable because they don't work, don't pay rent, and suffer from illiteracy. The mayor of the town initiating the effort defended it saying that "This wall is about one group that obeys the laws of the Czech Republic and behaves according to good morals, and about a group that breaks these rules–doesn't pay rent, doesn't use proper hygiene and doesn't do anything right. . . . This is not a racial problem. It is a problem of dealing with decent and indecent people." Another argued that "It's the culture; Romany (Gypsy) people are different." Another made the statement that "Complicating the issue is that the Gypsy community is quite diverse" (Perlez, 1998). Reflect back to the assertion that being different is often viewed as being synonymous with being wrong and therefore deviant, and that society creates outsiders. Recall also that it was stated that when members of the dominant populous makes a scapegoat of a peripheral group, accusing them of various forms of wrongdoing, that tends to serve as a prelude to later official and legal persecution.

With discrimination in the Czech Republic resulting in a 70 percent unemployment rate among Gypsies, rent delinquency is predictable. In Hungary, where discrimination reemerged following the collapse of communism, the Gypsies suffer a 90 percent unemployment rate, and discrimination in housing and education is also now acute. It is a self-fulfilling prophecy. Deprive a people of education, housing, and employment, and they will fail to live up to expected standards. Then, use that failure as verification that they are undesirable and as justification for discrimination in education, housing, and employment. It is no wonder why, in America, the Gypsies have chosen to be invisible. One elderly American Gypsy recalled how, when she was young and her migratory family was endeavoring to find work and settle down (she had become school age), they would be told to move along because their kind was not welcome. Historically, Gypsies were considered to be thieves but when a people are deprived the means to earn a living subsistence thievery is predictable. Again, a self fulfilling prophesy; deny them the means to earn a living (education and jobs) and they will steal, then use their having stolen as justification to deny them a job–what reasonable person would employ a thief?

America, being geographically so large, having a large population, containing so many varied cultures, and with less government control over issues such as housing, Gypsies have found it relatively easy to remain invisible by passing as some other nationality and blending with the socioeconomic background. However, in Europe that is not so easily accomplished. "Although their economic relationship to mainstream society is essentially the same as that of British travelers, unlike the latter, American gypsies are an inconspicuous minority and not a particular target for social control agencies. The main reason for this is that they live in rented houses, primarily in low income areas, so that, outwardly, their culture does not appear different to that of other ethnic minorities living in the same areas. For this reason, they are not labeled as deviant" (Sibley, 1981). It should be noted that the preceeding statement remains accurate relative to many American gypsies who are to varying degrees migratory, but of the sedentary Gypsies this writer knows, many own their own home and while some are in low income areas, many are not.

Accepting for purposes of discussion that society does create outsiders, there is merit to examining further how that is done even though that was previously discussed in Chapter 5 under the sub-heading "Does Society Creates Outsiders"? The following discussion is not redundant with, but augments, previous discussion.

There are many ways that society creates outsiders. The government may officially declare a certain people to be outsiders and undesirable, or they may be indirect and subtle. Long ago, in Britain, much of the Gypsy population would occupy the rural areas much of the year working agricultural jobs. Today, mechanization has eliminated much of the work they did and they have out of necessity gravitated to the cities with some very real problems resulting. But, legislation has also caused many of the problems.

Long ago, when travel was by means of horse drawn vehicles (caravans), Gypsies would take work along the way and as a result their mental geography was continuous. Today, however, because there are few jobs to be found along the way, their mental geography is a series of disjointed urban centers. Also, a factor is a significantly expanded range that is made possible by pulling their trailers with vehicles rather than horses.

While mechanization has driven the Gypsies from the countryside and into the cities, government legislation has also driven them into the cities, as stated. The *1959 Highways Act* made it illegal to camp beside the road or in a rest area. Also, since 1960 farmers could no longer permit Gypsies to camp on their land because the law required landowners to provide conventional toilets (flush toilets) and water for any caravan dwellers living on their property. That has served to diminish if not eliminate Gypsy access to any remaining agricultural jobs that had not been eliminated by mechanization. To make matters worse, the *1986 Public Order Act* has empowered the police to evict Gypsies from private land without first receiving a complaint from the land owner, and they are empowered to summarily arrest Gypsies who resist. The underlying intent of such laws is suspect, if not obvious. There would seem to be parallels with American laws regarding vagrancy.

Expansion of Britain's suburbs, and modern highways, has eliminated many traditional campsites, and many have purposely been eliminated. Although the *1968 Caravan Sites Act* requires local authorities to construct official campsites for all Gypsies residing in or resorting to their area, only partial compliance has been realized leaving over half the traveling Gypsies with no legal place to camp (George Gmelch & Sharon Gmelch, February 1988). Again we see a self-fulfilling prophecy; impose laws eliminating places to camp, and fail to honor the laws requiring construction of official (legal) campsites, and problems of illegal camping predictably result. To be sure, there are very real problems faced by settled people because of illegal Gypsy camping, but the source of the problem must be recognized. If a law causes a certain people to become a social problem, or seriously aggravates an existing problem, the tendency of the larger and settled population is to view the people in question with contempt and overlook the laws that caused them to become a problem, and to accept or overlook any subsequent laws targeting them. In a very real sense such laws result in increased bias towards a people and acceptance of the laws that unfairly target them.

The holocaust was preceded by a campaign to convince the public that the Jewish population was undesirable and the source of many social problems so that their annihilation if not condoned would at least be overlooked. They became scapegoats. And, the holocaust targeted Gypsies as well as Jews. To be sure, if Gypsies simply permitted themselves to be assimilated, or at least reduced to mimicking the lifestyle of the settled population, many of the problems would cease to exist. But, if that is the intent, would that not be a way to succeed where the holocaust failed? Would it not eradicate a culture? "Where centuries of persecution have failed, bureaucracy might just succeed in the final destruction of the gypsies" (Worral, 1979).

Today, in Britain, for reasons stated, the Gypsies are more nomadic than ever before. One could argue that the laws that have been enacted to curtail their nomadic ways have actually served to increase it. With no place to legally camp, problems caused by their illegal camping are predictable with evictions for illegal camping being frequent thus forcing them to move on, to resume a nomadic posture. Many Gypsies argue that the only time they are legal is when they are in motion traveling from one place to another or in a "designated" campsite, which are in short supply. That situation is reminiscent of the American homeless who have argued that to avoid a confrontation with police and business owners they must keep moving. Once they stop they are at risk. Again we see a self-fulfilling prophecy. Declare a people and their lifestyle as being aberrant and enact laws that disrupt their lifestyle with the resulting problems used as verification that the laws were justified.

The authors are not picking on the countries mentioned here, but using them to illustrate a situation. America has been guilty of enacting repressive legislation targeting the Gypsies, and failing to enforce laws that serve to protect them, although not nearly to the extent that occurs in other countries because Gypsies have chosen to be invisible; out of sight, out of mind!

There was a time when Asians (Chinese and later Japanese) were the subjects of severe repressive legislation, as blacks and Gypsies were and in too many cases still are. In some states it was illegal for a non-Asian to marry an Asian; an Asian not born in the United States could not become a citizen or own property; no further immigration of Asians was permitted unless they had family members already residing in the United States; Asians could not become members of labor unions and as a result worked for about half the wage of their unionized non-Asian coworkers. It was not until 1965 that United States immigration quotas ceased to restrict people based on their national origin. The list could go on.

In early years when labor was need, for the building of railroads for example, Asian immigration was encouraged and they were tolerated. But, once their labor was no longer needed they suffered serious intolerance, even to the extent of government shutting down their legitimate businesses. That is reminiscent of the railroad police being lenient towards train riding boes heading for Wenatchee, Washington, when harvest is pending and their labor needed, but being intolerant once harvest is over and their labor no longer essential. It is not possible for an Asian to conceal his or her ethnicity, as most blacks can't, but Gypsies are fortunate in that they are able to do so and they do it well. As a matter of policy Gypsies will admit their ethnicity to no one (non-Gypsies) as history continues to demonstrate that ethnic anonymity is fundamental to avoiding discrimination and persecution.

America's former President Clinton, in a State of the Union address, vowed that more funding would be provided for EEO enforcement. While that determination may be sincere, it only addresses part of the problem and the Gypsies (and other minorities) likely won't believe it until history proves otherwise. President Clinton also stated that the next census would seek an accurate count but, as in the past, the Gypsies will not be reflected for almost none will be willing to disclose their heritage. They will not trust the information to be used for statistical purposes only, regardless of such assurances. Truthful reporting would result in a government computer containing the identity and address of every United States Gypsy and to them that would be unacceptable and horrifying. That is understandable considering what was done to them before and during the holocaust and the history of repressive legislation, discrimination, and persecution that has followed in so many countries and continues to be practiced. They will remain invisible by claiming to be some other nationality with their numbers remaining seriously under reported while the numbers of other classes continue to be over reported to a corresponding degree. In the final analysis, while government figures reflect a limited United States Gypsy population, their numbers are significant.

Understandably, the effort to remain obscure is not evidenced only by their failure to be reflected on immigration and census records, but other official records as well. For example, when an old Gypsy man was killed in an automobile accident, his youngest son who at the time was in his late twenties provided the information reflected on the death certificate. The death certificate reflects the following questions and responses:

Color or Race: White
Birthplace: Unknown
Father's Name: Unknown
Mother's Maiden Name: Unknown
Marital Status: Widowed
Name of Husband or Wife: Left blank
Occupation: Farmer (retired)
Kind of Business or Industry: Diversified
If Veteran, Name War: Unknown
Social Security Number: Unknown
Name of Cemetery or Crematory: Unknown

The death certificate reflects who died, when, where, and how, with all genealogical information having been withheld. Also, the date of birth reflected on the death certificate is slightly different than reflected in family records. The fact that information was being selectively withheld is apparent inasmuch as the family has ancestral records that even include, in some instances, the names of cherished horses and other stock, the records dating back sufficiently far (8th great grand parent) as to identify one who arrived on the Mayflower in 1620, identifies those who participated in the Civil War, those who migrated to avoid the Civil War, one who was a regular on *The Lawrence Welk Show* for years, etc. But, by withholding information where official documents are concerned the normal paper trail that one leaves in life is left incomplete and therefore ambiguous.

Considering that an outsider's understanding of Gypsies has never been used for their benefit, but to their detriment, remaining cryptic would seem to be proper and fitting. The determination to remain cryptic is also evidenced by the tombstone of another Gypsy, the stone reflecting what is alleged to be his true surname followed by the fictitious surname he used in life; his alias. But, in that case, those outside the culture will never know with certainty whether the "true surname" is not itself a family alias for it is common for Gypsies to adopt surnames characteristic of the country in which they reside. A Gypsy once made the statement, relative to inquiries made by outsiders, "Ask ten Gypsies the same question and you will get ten different answers. Ask the same Gypsy the same question ten times and you will get ten different answers." History has demonstrated that anonymity is fundamental to avoiding discrimination and persecution, and anonymity is an art they have out of necessity mastered.

While Gypsies are significant in number, far more than realized by the government, and the subjects of discrimination and persecution, very few seek legal recourse when discriminated against. One EEOC representative, when receiving a complaint from a Gypsy relative to employment discrimination, did not know if they were a protected class. She had to investigate to make that determination and found a Supreme Court ruling declaring Gypsies to be a protected class. Only then was the complaint accepted. Her confusion was based on the fact that they have no country. So, if they are a protected class, and subjected to considerable discrimination and persecution, why do so few seek legal recourse? The answer is simply that so doing runs counter to their determination to remain cryptic, and why sacrifice anonymity in favor of a suit that has the possibility of being unsuccessful? When one Gypsy filed a lawsuit in response to a police search and the confiscation of jewelry and money, he encountered considerable resistance from the Gypsy community who preferred that the loss be suffered in silence so as to retain their anonymity.

For those who don't understand, it is convenient to believe that a cryptic posture has been assumed for the purpose of facilitating criminal activity. But, when a history of discrimination and persecution has taught a class of people that being cryptic is an appropriate defense, the only viable defense, the members who are criminal (who are a minority of the group) will find that being cryptic is an asset in that respect. Also, when a class of people has suffered a history of discrimination and persecution at the hands of the dominant society, and their government, being discriminated against relative to employment, education, and housing, it is understandable why some (not the majority) would to varying degrees begin to see the system of the dominant society as being there to be exploited.

Those who discriminate can be said to have created a situation whereby they become "fair game" for exploitation, in the minds of the oppressed. The issue becomes clear when viewing it within the context of the dynamics of employee theft, acknowledging that the ingredients necessary for employee theft to occur are (1) need, (2) desire, (3) opportunity, and (4) rationalization. The employee who steals from the employer, because they must daily "return to the scene of the crime," to lessen the feeling of guilt must find a way to rationalize their conduct and make it justified in their own mind. The employee may justify it by arguing (in their own mind) that they are entitled to the proceeds of theft because they are under paid, were unjustly denied a promotion, are not afforded adequate benefits, etc. In many respects, those who discriminate against a class of people create the need, desire, and the means for rationalization. All that remains is to find and exploit the opportunity.

There are many who condemn Black people for a history of receiving government assistance (welfare) feeling that they are unjustly exploiting the system. However, by no measure are all Black people guilty of that, and there are also white people, and people of other races and nationalities, receiving government assistance. But, as for Blacks who do receive government assistance, what is the root of the problem? There are many reasons but it remains a fact that their children continue to attend poorly funded schools, and discrimination in employment and housing remains a fact. There is a problem when Black children are told to study diligently so they can get a good education and succeed in the labor market, but are simultaneously provided inadequately funded schools, and they know that job discrimination remains a fact. As for Gypsies, it will never be known by the dominant society to what extent a parallel situation exists because they are largely invisible. But, it would be fair to say that many feel little or no loyalty to a society that has created the need to maintain a cryptic posture.

As should be apparent, the Gypsy ability to read people is something that has of necessity been cultivated from a very early age. And, not being part of the dominant society on whose fringes they live, their view of that society has not been distorted by being a part of it; they view it from a social distance. Having historically been a traveling and persecuted people surviving by their wits and intuitions, many have accumulated a vast and unique frame of reference, an understanding of the world and the people around them that members of settled society cannot fathom, a view that should be the envy of any sociologist, a view that has not been diminished and distorted by assimilation and luxury. That contrasts sharply with the assertion of one writer who claimed that American Gypsies are almost universally illiterate and completely unaware of current events. While many American Gypsies continue to practice traditional self-employment occupations characteristic of their predecessors, many are employed in blue-collar trades, many occupy white collar professional positions, many own their own business, and there are some this writer is aware of who have achieved high level positions in academia, and in the sciences.

Gypsies have and continue to live in a harsh world of reality that requires viewing the world as it is, the harshness of their world contrasting sharply with the often romantic view that settled people have of them. Historically mainstream people have enjoyed their magic, the jewelry they make, their fortune-telling, and their music, and many have benefited from their enviable skills in animal husbandry, but heaven forbid they move in next door. When viewed from a distance they can be seen as mysterious, romantic, and interesting, but when viewed up close their lifestyle and values are seen as different and therefore aberrant and bias becomes an overriding factor. Being at variance with the dominant value system they quickly become labeled as deviant and relegated to the status of outsider, and treated accordingly. That is understandable because it is human nature to accept that which is liked, understood, and is consistent with one's own values and beliefs, but to reject that which opposes and therefore challenges one's values and beliefs. That people tend to resent and resist opposing views is apparent when listening to a debate over topics such as religion and politics.

While Gypsies do not internalize the values and norms of settled society, they understand them very well. And, members of ethnic and cultural minority groups who are able to conceal their status by means of grooming and dress, for purposes of employment, are uniquely aware of bias because they experience the contrast between how they are treated when they are on the job appearing to be mainstream versus when off the job and not appearing to be mainstream.

Although in the United States there remain many traveling Gypsies, many have become sedentary out of necessity. One significant factor diminishing travel is the requirement that their children attend school. But, for many, being sedentary is difficult and one man, who with his family had been migratory until the firstborn reached school age, always kept a travel trailer behind his house. When one of his grand-son's asked his mother (the man's daughter), relative to the trailer, if grandpa still periodically traveled, she replied, "No, he likes to sit in his trailer and read." For that man the trailer was his connection to the past, the migratory life he obviously missed.

Before proceeding it would be worthwhile to mention that just because a class of people are migratory does not mean they do not reg-ularly take traditional employment even though temporary, or that they are in any way a detriment to settled society. A migratory American Gypsy family this writer visited with recently consisted of the parents and three young adult children, two sons, and a daughter. They traveled by motor home and when money was nearing depletion they would rent a space in a low rent RV Park (Recreational Vehicle Park in an economically disadvantaged part of town) and everyone would find jobs. While sedentary the parents lived in the motor home while the two sons and daughter shared a large tent that was parti-tioned with two chests of drawers and drapery. The sons occupied one side while the daughter occupied the other. All five family members would go forth and secure jobs and, although each obtained a low pay-ing job, when the money was consolidated the family income was sub-stantial, especially when compared against their low cost of living. When funds had been sufficiently replenished they would move on. Their way of life, although different from that of the mainstream majority, is a life they are content with and they are in no way a detri-ment to the society on whose fringes they live.

Today, in the United States, while many Gypsies have become sedentary, not to be confused with assimilated, there are more travel-ing Gypsies than is generally realized. The prolific use of motor homes and travel trailers by mainstream people has helped them remain obscure even while traveling. Although originally emigrating from India between 800 and 950 A.D., generations of intermarriage with outsiders and with other nomadic people has lightened their skin, and they have adopted surnames characteristic of the country in which they reside. Those two factors make it easier to avoid racial detection.

Most members of settled society who have contact with Gypsies, and most do, do so not realizing it. An American sociologist, who attempted to study them, in a published treatise, acknowledged that he had gained only a small glimpse into their inner world, their culture and economies. He saw only what he was permitted to see. Logically, he concluded that their society is so elusive, closed, and cryptic, that by comparison they make the Mafia look like an open society. Hence, stereotypes and myths persist. For reasons stated, Gypsies remain profoundly distrustful of government and socially distanced from outsiders (non-Gypsies or, gauje).

APPENDICES

Appendix 1

A HOBO KINGS PERCEPTION OF GYPSIES

Parents all over the country told their children that the Gypsies would steal kids. What a lie. This created such hatred in growing kids. Lord have mercy on our narrow-minded predecessors. They caused a great race of people untold misery.

Steam Train Maury Graham

In Chapter 6 considerable information was provided regarding a little known culture, Gypsies. The following is one page from a self-published book written by the legendary Maury Graham, a.k.a. Steam Train, five times elected King of the Hoboes, a man who has spent the larger portion of his long life traveling the country riding the trains (freight trains) and working miscellaneous jobs. His perspective is interesting and enlightening and nicely augments the preceding discussion of the Gypsy culture.

"I'm not an authority on Gypsies, so this will be a short chapter. There has been plenty said in the past, but maybe not enough.

"These people came into the country as immigrants before and around the turn of the century. Their origin is still a puzzle to many. They were a colorful nation of people coming from Romania, Hungary, Yugoslavia, and some other Mediterranean places. They were seeking freedom and a place under the sun. Being a nomadic people made them different from other foreigners arriving in this country. They could be considered one of the earliest types of vagabond, from the old times.

"When they hit the shore here, they saw a beautiful land that one could roam in and live off. Why bunch up when there were such wide open spaces ahead just a few miles? So, getting their horses and building the first mobile homes, they started.

"They loved their horses and were experts on them. Many made their living by training, selling, and trading. Long before coming to the United States, they were very knowledgeable of horses. With their horsemanship, they could capture any crowd in any town or hamlet.In the early twenties expert horse people told me that Gypsies were the best horsemen in the world at training and handling. Some said they believed Gypsies could talk to horses. They trained horses for riding and for work in the harness by kindness and talking, not by 'breaking them.' They also cured many an ailing horse for farmers and cowboys.

"The Gypsies' wagons were handmade and a beautiful work of art, with intricate woodcarvings. There were several trades connected in making the wagons. Across the country they plied their trades and crafts. For their own self-protection they traveled in large clans. Luckily so, because, sorry to say, our early settlers were practicing what the Gypsies had run away from, prejudice. They tell me that there are still small pockets of it around the country. I hope not.

"However, stiff-necked people in some communities resented this free group. They threw stones at them and rallied against them. Because they were different, people persecuted them in many ways. Such a carefree colorful people! Their religion upset many because it varied from others.

"I remember my own folks telling me back in the early twenties 'Don't go near those people. They steal children.' The Gypsies always had a bunch of their own. Parents all over the country told their children that the Gypsies would steal kids. What a lie. This created such hatred in growing kids. Lord have mercy on our narrow-minded predecessors. They caused a great race of people untold misery. Because of this prejudice, the Gypsies had to be shrewd to exist and steal to keep from starving. Well, this didn't make friends either.

"Just before World War, II the Gypsy began to settle down in the cities, mostly in the East. It's the changing times again.

"When I was a boy, I always loved their beautiful horses stepping high, and their fine painted wagons, as they passed our place in Kansas. Alas, the vagabond Gypsy has gone the way of other vagabonds, regimented in the cities" (Steam Train Maury Graham– 1985).

Appendix 2

WAR CHIEF JOSEPH'S SPEECH IN WASHINGTON, D.C.

Treat all men alike. Give them all the same law. Give them all an even chance to live and grow. All men were made by the same Great Spirit Chief. They are all brothers. The earth is the mother of all people and all people should have equal rights upon it.

War Chief Joseph

This book has discussed many aspects of the problem of discrimination and persecution, but the American Indian has not been discussed to any significant degree. But, it must be acknowledged that they have suffered severe discrimination, persecution, and even acts of genocide, from the time the "White man" began settling the U.S. Although this book was not intended to delve into American history except as it incidentally pertains to discrimination, or to delve into the history of the American Indian, there is a great deal of valuable historical social insight to be gleaned from the articulate speech that the Nez Perce Indian, War Chief Joseph (1840?–1904), made in Washington, D.C., subsequent to the Nez Perce war of 1877. His speech addresses the consistent failure thereafter of the government to honor the surrender agreement while cruelly subjecting the Indian people to extreme oppression.

War Chief Joseph so eloquently delivered the following speech.

"I believe General Miles would have kept his word if he could have done so. I do not blame him for what we have suffered since the surrender. I do not know who is to blame. We gave up our horses, over 1,100, and our saddles, over 100. And we have not heard from them since. Somebody has got our horses.

137

"General Miles turned my people over to another soldier and we were taken to Bismarck. Captain Johnson, who now had charge of us, received an order to take us to Fort Leavenworth. At Leavenworth we were placed on a low river bottom with no water except river water to drink and cook with. We had always lived in a healthy country where the mountains were high and the water was cold and clear. Many of my people sickened and died, and we buried them in this strange land. I cannot tell how much my heart suffered for my people while at Leavenworth. The Great Spirit Chief who rules above seemed to be looking some other way and did not see what was being done to my people.

"During the hot days we received notice that we were to be moved farther away from our own country. We were not asked if we were willing to go. We were ordered to get into the railroad cars. Three of my people died on the way to Baxter Springs. It was worse to die there than to die fighting in the mountains. We were moved from Baxter Springs to Indian Territory (now the state of Oklahoma) and set down without our lodges. We had but little medicine and we were nearly all sick. Seventy of my people have died since we moved here. We have had a great many visitors who have talked many ways. Some of the Chiefs from Washington came to see us, and selected land for us to live upon. We have not moved to that land for it is not a good place to live. The commissioner Chief came to see us. I told him, as I told everyone, that I expected General Miles word would be carried out. He said it could not be done, that White men must live in my country and all the land was taken up, that if I returned to Wallowa, I could not live in peace, that law papers were out against young men who began the war and that the government could not protect my people. This talk feel like a heavy stone upon my heart. I saw that I could not gain anything by talking to him. Other law chiefs came to see me and said they would help me to get a healthy country. I did not know who to believe. The White people have too many chiefs. They do not understand each other, and do not talk alike. The Commissioner Chief invited me to go with him and hunt for a better home than we have now. I like the land we found west of the Osage Reservation, better than any place I have seen in the country, but it is not a healthy land. There are no mountains and rivers, the water is warm, it is not a good country for stock. I do not believe my people can live there. I am afraid that we will all die. The Indians who occupy that country are dying off. I promised Chief Hayes (President Rutherford B. Hayes) to go there and do the best I could until the government got ready to make good General Miles word. I was not satisfied but I could not help myself. Then the Inspector Chief came to my camp and we had a long talk. He said I ought to have a home in the mountain country north and that we could write a letter to the Great Chief in Washington. Again the hope of seeing the mountains of Idaho and Oregon grew up in my heart.

"At last I was granted permission to come to Washington and bring my friend Yellow Bull and our interpreter with me. I am glad we came. I have shaken hands with a great many friends, but there are some things I want to know which no one seems able to explain. I cannot understand how the government sends a man out to fight us as he did General Miles and then breaks his word. Such a government has something wrong with it. I cannot understand why so many chiefs are allowed to speak so many different ways, and promise so many different things. I have seen the Great Father Chief (President Rutherford B. Hayes), the next great chief, the Commissioner Chief, the Law Chief, and many other law chiefs, and they all say they are my friends and that I shall have justice. But while their mouths all talk right I do not understand why nothing is done for my people. I have heard talk and talk but nothing is done. Good words do not last long unless they amount to something. Words do not pay for my dead people. They do not pay for my country, now overrun by White men. They do not protect my father's grave. They do not pay for all my horses and cattle. Good words will not give me back my children. Good words will not make good the promise of your War Chief General Miles. Good words will not give my people good health and stop them from dying. Good words will not get my people a home, where they can live in peace and take care of themselves. I am tired of talk that comes to nothing. It makes my heart sick when I remember all the good words and all the broken promises. There has been too much talking by men who have no right to talk. Too many misrepresentations have been made. Too many misunderstandings have come up between the White men about the Indians. If the White man wants to live in peace with the Indians he can live in peace. There need be no trouble. Treat all men alike. Give them all the same law. Give them all an even chance to live and grow. All men were made by the same Great Spirit Chief. They are all brothers. The earth is the mother of all people and all people should have equal rights upon it. You might as well expect the rivers to run backwards as that any man who was born a free man should be contented when penned up and denied liberty to go where he pleases. If you tie a horse to a stake do you expect he will grow fat? If you pen an Indian up on a small spot of earth and compel him to stay there he will not be content, nor will he grow and prosper. I have asked some of the great White chiefs where they get their authority to say to the Indian that he shall stay in one place while he sees other White men going where they please. They cannot tell me. I only ask of the government to be treated as all other men are treated. If I cannot go to my own home let me have a home in some country where my people will not die so fast. I would like to go to Bitter Root Valley. There my people would be healthy. Where they are now they are dying. Three have died since I left my camp to come to Washington. When I think of our condition my heart is heavy. I see men of my race treated as outlaws and driven from country to country or shot down like animals. I know that my race must change. We cannot hold our own with the White men as we are. We only ask an even chance to live as other men live. We ask to be recognized as men. We ask that the same law shall work alike on all men. If the Indian breaks the law, punish him by the law. If the White man breaks the law, punish him also. Let me be a free man—free to travel, free to stop, free to work, free to trade where I choose, free to choose my own teachers, free to follow the religion of my fathers, free to think and talk and act for myself, and I will obey every law or submit to the penalty. Whenever the White man treats the Indian as they treat each other, then we will all have no more wars. We shall all be alike, brothers of one father and one mother, with one sky above us and one country around us, and one government for all. Then the Great Spirit Chief who rules above will smile upon this land, and send rain to wash out the bloody spots made by brothers' hands from the face of the earth. For this time the Indian race are waiting and praying. I hope that no more groans of wounded men and children will ever go to the ear of the Great Spirit Chief above, and that all people may be one people.

In-mut-too-yah-lat-lat has spoken for his people."

BIBLIOGRAPHY

Aether Systems' Mobile Government Division. (2001). "Special Report II: Racial Profiling: Overcoming the Perception of Racial Profiling." *Law and Order, 49,* (4).

Appelbaum, Richard P. & William J. Chambliss. (1995). *Sociology.* New York, NY: Harper Collins College Publishers.

Carnes, Jim. (1995). *Us and Them, A History of Intolerance in America.* Teaching Tolerance, Montgomery, Alabama. (Supplement guide to the video, The Shadow of Hate).

David, Sibley. (1981). *Outsiders in Urban Societies.* New York, NY: St. Martin's Press.

Douglas, John, & Mark Olshaker. (1995). *Mind Hunter.* New York, NY: Simon & Schuster, Inc.

Edwards, Eric. (2001). *Racial Profiling: Issues and Law.* Arizona: City of Phoenix Police Department.

Gmelch, George, & Sharon Gmelch. (1988). "Nomads in the Cities," *Natural History magazine,* 97, (2).

Guggenheim, Charles. (1995). *The Shadow of Hate, A History of Intolerance in America.* Teaching Tolerance, Montgomery, Alabama.

Hansen, Ron, &Carl Milazzo. (2000). *Race Relations in Police Operations: A Legal and Ethical Perspective.* Arizona: Chiefs of Police conference.

Hendricks, James E., & Bryan Byers. (2000). *Multicultural Perspectives In Criminal Justice And Criminology* (2nd ed). Springfield, IL: Charles C Thomas Publisher, LTD.

Hennessy, Stephen M., Douglas F. Warring, Myrna Cornett-DeVito, James Arnott, & Gerald H. Heuett. (2000). *A Cultural Awareness Trainer's Manual for Law Enforcement Officers* (5th ed). Scottsdale, AZ: Leadership Publishing.

Hennessy, Stephen M. (1999). *Thinking Cop Feeling Cop* (3rd ed). Gainsville, FL: Center for Applications of Psychological Type, Inc.

House of Commons Standing Committees. (1967-8). *Official Report* (6).

Howard, Helen Addison. (1941 & 1865). *Saga of Chief Joseph.* Caldwell, ID: The Caxton Printers, LTD. (University of Nebraska Press, Lincoln and London).

Jane Perlez. (1998). Journal: "Czech Gypsies Face Bias From Beyond the Wall".

Law Enforcement Television. (1993). Street Talk, Cultural Awareness. Louisiana Educational Media.

Mac Donald, Heather. (2001). "The Myth of Racial Profiling". *City-Journal, 11,* (2).

NewsBriefs. (1995). *Maryland Police Agree to End Racial Drug Courier Profiles.*

O'Connell, Dick. (2000). "Racial Profiling". *This Week In Law Enforcement.* Washington, D.C.

Ramirez, Deborah, Jack McDevitt, & Amy Farell. (2000). *A Resource Guide on Racial Profiling Data Collection Systems: Promising Practices and Lessons Learned.* Bonston, MA: Northeastern University, NCJ 184768.

Remsberg, Charles. (1995). *Tactics for Criminal Patrol.* Northbrook, IL: Caliber Press, Inc.

Senate Concurrent Resolution No. 111. (1999). State of New Jersey.

Steam Train Maury Graham. (1985). *A History of the Hoboes, Tramps, and Other Vagabonds.* (self-published).

Traffic Stops Statistics Study Act of 1999. (1999). United States Senate, 106th Congress.

Turvey. (1999). *Criminal Profiling: An Introduction to Behavioral Evidence* Analysis. San Diego, CA: Academic Press.

US v. Armstrong 517 U.S. 465, 116 S.Ct.1480 (1996).

US v. Avery 137 F.3d 343 (6th Cir. 1997).

INDEX